T3-BOE-521

DISCOUNT JUSTICE

The Canadian Criminal Justice System

DISCOUNT JUSTICE

Daniel Jay Baum

Burns & MacEachern Limited

BRESCIA COLLEGE
LIBRARY

42374

© 1979 by Burns & MacEachern Limited. All rights reserved.

Canadian Cataloguing in Publication Data

  Baum, Daniel Jay, 1934-
    Discount justice

Includes index.
ISBN 0-88768-080-1 pa.

1. Criminal justice, Administration of — Canada.
I. Title.

KE8200.B39   364'.971   C79-094067-1

ISBN 0-88768-080-1

Design: First Image/Michael Gray
Cover Illustration: Patrick Corrigan
Typesetting: Video Text, Barrie

Printed and bound in Canada

Contents

Preface

This is a book with a focus: it is directed toward the community. It asks what we can do to make the community a safe, peaceful and, above all, a free place in which to live. This book has been written not for specialists, not even for legislators, government officials or judges. It has been written for *citizens* in the belief that law can be understood by them, and that the people as a whole, rather than specialists, should and will decide what kind of law and law enforcement they want.

A detailed narrative note section forms a part of this book. It provides source materials and, in some instances, more detailed explanations of the statements made in the text.

There are many who helped in giving this book shape. Let me mention a few. Research assistance that included not only searching the law, but also determining how the law was being implemented in reality, was done by Michael O'Brien, a student completing his third year at Osgoode Hall Law School, and Linda Grobovsky, a Toronto social worker. Typing and retyping manuscript was the task of Maxine Yaskiw and Mrs. Naomi Kuhn. To all of them I express my deep thanks.

There is also a special note of thanks that I give to my publisher, B. D. Sandwell, who offered so much encouragement. In the final analysis, however, I bear full responsibility for that which has been written.

D. J. Baum
Osgoode Hall Law School
Toronto

CHAPTER ONE

Crime: Fear and Rage — an Overview

"The community . . . should participate and concern itself with the job prisons are doing, if for no other reason than for its own safety." **Canadian Parliamentary Committee Report, 1977.**

False, Unreasoning Fear: A Fortress Mentality

Who will answer the scream in the night? Who will safeguard the home and its contents? In the city, where most Canadians live, there can be, there often is, a sense of aloneness. Personal safety, the security of property, in the first instance is an individual responsibility — neighbours cannot be depended upon to help. Indeed, until about 1968 they could not even be depended upon to help the police. At that time special legislation was introduced in Ontario to compensate the "Good Samaritan" injured while assisting police in the performance of their duties. The law was designed to encourage citizens to be involved in crime prevention.

In the cities, however, citizen involvement in crime prevention has a very limited meaning. For the police it means those programmes in which persons act alone or in family groups to care for themselves. It means locks and keys and caution in moving about the city. Homes and cars are meant to be locked. Children are to be kept close to the home. Daughters are instructed what to wear so that they do not "encourage" strangers.

1

The assumption seems to be that criminals are on the loose. Given the opportunity to strike, there is little doubt what will happen — the citizen will be victimized. Except in the security of locked homes and cars citizens believe themselves to be at risk. The fear of crime has become a pervasive fact in Canadian life. The cost in human terms and money is staggering.

In periods of national emergency the government has never imposed on the Canadian population as a whole the restraints that Canadians have willingly placed on themselves. Day after day Canadians, both rich and poor, place curfews on themselves. They limit and intimidate their children by instilling fear of violence from unknown criminals. They restrict their own freedom to travel and meet others. They create and heighten the very feelings that led many of their parents and grandparents to leave their native land and seek Canada as a home. They do all this out of fear. More often than not, they seem to feel that crime cannot be combated except by erecting personal fortresses where each person waits alone and frightened.

Yet how curious it is. Those who fear are the majority by far. Those whom they fear are generally not violent. They commit crimes against property without acts of violence. Their backgrounds tend to be problem filled. They often are the product of broken families. Alcohol or other drugs frequently have played a heavy role in their lives. They can properly be called the "losers" in the community. They are those on the outside; they do not form a part of mainstream Canadian life.

Native Canadians, especially Indians, who have come into contact with mainstream Canada and suffered the disintegration of their tribal and family life, illustrate the point. A 1973 report by the Attorney General of British Columbia found that native Indians represent about 5 per cent of that province's total population. They account for 13 per cent of total admissions to British Columbia correctional institutions. This is but the tip of the problem. With only 5 per cent of the population Indians constitute 40 per cent of the children given into the custody of the province's protective Human Resources Department. The same lopsided statistics would apply to the problem of alcoholism. The point is that crime among the Indians, as with any other group, does not occur unrelated to life in the community.

A 1976 report prepared for the Law Reform Commission of Canada stated:

> Indian communities that are economically self-sufficient with a high degree of moral and social solidarity are rare. An example [in British Columbia] is the Nishka community, a small fishing settlement on an isolated northern coastal reserve. They have a prosperous and independent economy. They have a strong policing system of their

own, and have re-created some of the older tribal methods of social control. Such communities have no need of outside "help" or outside "justice."

In Canada crime is treated as unrelated to the rest of the community. It is a wrong in itself which demands some form of punishment. To carry out the public will, a veritable army of police has been established. In Canada we have one police officer for approximately every 500 persons. The maintenance of this criminal justice system, rivalling the armed forces, cost us in 1974 one and a half billion dollars.

Yet the system is not working. At any point in time there are about 20,000 Canadians behind bars. In the view of many, including the police, this is not nearly enough. The police know that not all convictions result in imprisonment. There are three reported crimes for every conviction. And for every offence reported, two are not. (For some offences, such as shoplifting, where the amounts involved are as little as ten dollars, only one in every ten offences is reported to the police.)

Neither deterrence nor rehabilitation seem to be the operative goals of the criminal justice system. In federal prisons, housing those convicted of the more serious crimes, the average sentence for one convicted of breaking and entering is about fourteen months. The actual time spent in prison is likely to be less than ten months. The law remits one-third of the sentence as a reward for good behaviour, and then permits release on parole at an early stage of the sentence.

The "repeater" rate, or recidivism, ranges between 60 and 80 per cent. That is, 60 to 80 per cent of those released from prison will eventually return to prison as punishment for another offence against the Crown. This will happen whether the punishment is dark and silent isolation, or serving time in enlightened prisons.

Some think the problem of crime and the criminal can be pushed aside. More prisons can be built. Longer sentences can be meted out. There can even be a return to the days of beatings, hosings, manacles and starvation diets. There can be an end to work-release programmes. Let the convicted be imprisoned, isolated and, above all, punished.

The difficulty with such a community response is that the problem remains. In the 1960s and 1970s Canadian prisons seethed with violence. Hostages were taken and property destroyed. Violence only seemed to bring more violence. And the cost of maintaining a prisoner in a federal institution rose to over $17,000 annually. There was approximately one prison official for every prisoner.

A Canadian parliamentary committee was struck, consisting of members of all parties. In 1977 its report was submitted to the House of Commons, and left for consideration by the government. This is what the committee said about community participation:

No penitentiary service can succeed without understanding and participation by the public. Prisons belong to the public and therefore the people who pay for them have a vested interest in their remaining peaceful and in serving their best interests. Also those who enter prisons as offenders are born of the community and their damage is caused within the community. Thus the community has a vested interest in sharing in the prisoner's reform. The community also should participate and concern itself with the job the prisons are doing, if for no other reason than for its own safety. The best protection society has is for those who offend to come out of prison, not as a greater danger to the community, but as law-abiding, productive and tax-paying instead of tax-draining.

The Face of Crime

Canadians have not been involved in shaping the criminal justice system. They have left that job to so-called specialists. And the specialists have been found wanting. Crimes against property have not been stopped; they have not even been slowed considerably. (Violent crimes have not increased in recent years. Yet this may not be a result of effective law enforcement; it may relate rather to a population that is growing older. Violent crime tends to be committed by the young. The large numbers of teenagers and young adults of the "baby boom" years are passing into older adult status, and the level of violent crime accordingly is lessening.)

From arrest, to trial, to imprisonment, the system has largely failed. The 1977 parliamentary report stated:

There is little in the system to stimulate inmates to reform, to correct the behaviour and morality that brought them into prison. Thus the Canadian Penitentiary Service has failed the Canadians who paid highly and must continue to pay for reformative processes that they can only hope can succeed inside the big wall. . . . Most of those in prison are not dangerous. However, cruel lockups, isolation, the injustices and harassment deliberately inflicted on prisoners unable to fight back, make non-violent inmates violent, and those already dangerous more dangerous.

What the parliamentary committee said of the prison system applies to all facets of the criminal justice system.

The most serious price paid by Canadians for non-involvement in the criminal justice system is fear, unfounded and unreasoning fear. Crime becomes the unspeakable nightmare about which nothing can be done. Instead of facing that fear and dealing with crime as the community problem which it is, Canadians are encouraged by law enforcement officers to become defensive, to wall themselves away from their neighbours and their community. Such an approach does not make the problem of fighting crime less severe. Rather, it heightens isolation in already large and complex cities. It breeds mistrust and irrationality. It allows the Law Reform Commission of Canada to say in its 1976 report: "Fear of crime is natural. Of all the things that frighten us — accidents, diseases, natural disasters — crime has a particular place. It wears a human face. Other things happen. A crime is done deliberately. Hijacking, bombing, kidnapping and so on do not just occur, they are planned. And planned increasingly perhaps: at any rate there is a growing sense in Canada and many other countries of crisis about crime. Small wonder crime brings fear."

It is worth pausing for a moment to note that the fear of crime does not exist in the same way throughout Canada. And in some communities throughout the world it does not seem to exist at all. A recent immigrant from Finland who lives with her three children in suburban Toronto said: "My neighbours sometimes are angry with me. I live alone with my children. I never lock my door. I did not do this in my native country. There was never any reason to do so. We did not fear crime, and I do not choose to fear it in this country. But my neighbours become upset with me. They do not like to have their children play with mine at home if the door is not locked. They do not like it when I allow my children to go by bus to the shopping centre without an adult. They do not want their daughters to go along because they do not think it is safe. I believe this is their problem. Nothing has happened to my children. I want them to feel safe and they do."

The new immigrant refuses to be intimidated by fear of crime. But would she feel the same if she had lived in the area of Regent Park, close to Toronto's Yonge Street Strip where twelve-year-old Emanuel Jaques was murdered in the summer of 1977? Emanuel lived in Regent Park and worked the streets as a shoeshine boy. His parents were immigrants from the Portuguese Azores where crimes of violence are rare. Emanuel was the victim of sexual abuse and murder. His body was found stuffed in a garbage bag on the roof of one of the Strip's massage parlours.

The murder of one boy reached many parents. The Reverend Harold Jackman, a pastor in Regent Park, said of his twelve-year-old daughter: "I cannot let her stray too far from home now and I think every other parent here is as worried as I am." And indeed they were worried. Children were kept on a leash, confined to their neighbourhood. They were no longer left to explore the city, to visit Ontario Place or the Canadian National Exhibition. In the words of a school board trustee who lives in Regent Park, "everyone will become more withdrawn."

That same fear expressed itself in anger. Fifteen thousand of the Portuguese community marched on City Hall and demanded more power to the police. They wanted the Strip shut down. They blamed the porno houses, the massage parlours, and the general air of permissiveness that permeated the Strip for the death of Emanuel. And they wanted the killers found, tried, and convicted. They wanted the community as a whole to stigmatize the wrong.

And the police, the regulatory agencies, the city, and the province acted. Systematic raids took place. Zoning, building, and health codes were rigorously enforced. A special prosecutor was named and his staff appointed. Police were seen everywhere on the Strip. Arrests for loitering or soliciting became frequent. The cost of enforcement no longer seemed a problem. Even the courts "co-operated," if that term may be used. Indeed, David Crombie, the mayor of Toronto, gave principal credit to the courts, which issued injunctions and meted out stiff penalties rather than the light fines of years past. The courts also permitted application of an almost forgotten provincial law allowing padlocking of premises whose occupants in the previous three months had been convicted of running a "disorderly house." Political pressure, too, was placed on otherwise respectable landlords who had closed their eyes to the activities taking place in their buildings in order to take in high rents from sex activities.

Susan Fish, a member of Toronto City Council, put the matter well: "There was nothing done to clean up Yonge Street that could not have been done previously. There was no legal impediment that was taken out of the way to permit the authorities to do what they did. . . . Sad to say, the tide really turned with the killing of the Jaques boy and the inflaming of public opinion."

Yet, it was not the Toronto community that rose and demanded the closing of the Yonge Street Strip. While the larger community might have been shocked by the murder of Emanuel Jaques, it certainly was not frightened. It did not feel the same intimidation as the neighbourhood of Regent Park. What did happen was political action by government. That action could be taken because government no longer had to concern itself with a political backlash from the majority if the Strip were closed. In effect, the murder of the Jaques boy had neutralized the majority and allowed government to act.

The action taken by government had little to do with rational community debate. As a rational matter it can hardly be said that the Strip was, as such, responsible for the death of Emanuel Jaques. His murder could have taken place anywhere. The attack on the Strip became a way to vent the frustration, hurt, fear and anger of Portuguese-Canadians. Suppose the murderers of Emanuel Jaques had been caught, tried, convicted, and executed within twenty-four hours of the boy's death. Would the Portuguese community have demanded the closing of the Strip? Would the remainder of the community have been as silent in the face of government action? After all, wasn't the Strip a favourite place for many in the city?

In the case of Emanuel Jaques, government used the boy's murder and the criminal law to act in a way which would have been difficult in the normal exercise of political debate. The government played upon the emotions of a hurt group and the silence of the majority. This was an abuse of the democratic process; it certainly cannot be said to have been the result of community action.

Government did not use the death of Emanuel Jaques to open debate either on whether the Strip should be maintained, or into the underlying causes of the boy's death. Government did not exercise leadership in helping to develop responsible community action. Rather, government used the moment to achieve an end.

Perhaps the arrest and trial of those charged with the murder of the boy at least could have vindicated the community's shared belief that murder was to be condemned. The community had reason to expect this. The statistics show that while the annual rate of homicide in Canada has more than doubled between 1961 and 1976 (from 1.27 to 2.90 per 100,000 residents), the police clearance rate has remained at about 90 per cent (a figure far higher than that relating to crimes against property). The community was not disappointed either in the quality or speed of the police investigation. Homicide detectives moved swiftly. Four men were arrested and charged with the murder of Emanuel. The police wanted convictions; they thought they had done their work well; they expected the criminal process to reflect what they had done; they expected the Crown to carry forward successfully the case against the four.

The trial was the place where fundamental values were to be affirmed. The accused were to have the benefit of trial by jury, a right won in 1215 through the Magna Carta, and now largely eliminated in most criminal trials involving so-called "minor offences" because it is expensive. They were to stand in the dock behind their lawyers and be tried. The issue was not complex: Did they knowingly cause the death of Emanuel Jaques?

A Morality Play? — The Criminal Trial

For the public the charge of murder is clear, despite some subtlety in the degrees of murder. Yet what does the public really know of this event called a trial? It determines guilt or innocence. It is formal; it can even be called a ritual. The trial mystifies; evidence is received only if elaborate rules designed chiefly to protect the accused are followed. The trial is a pageant with roles acted by persons in gowns who alone fully comprehend the play. Indeed, the rules for the pageant were

7

formed by the actors, the professionals, both barristers and judges, over the centuries.

The Law Reform Commission of Canada said in 1976: "If criminal law has to do with affirming fundamental values, the criminal trial is *par excellence* the place where this is done. The trial is not just directed at the offender in the dock or even at potential offenders outside. On the contrary, it is a public demonstration to denounce the crime and re-affirm the values it infringed. It is . . . a sort of morality play for all of us. The trial is a kind of public theatre in the round."

The trial may be theatre, but it surely is not conducted before the public. Only a few can be seated in the courtroom. Television cameras are not permitted. Reports to the public come from the press which exercises its own sifting process, determined in no small measure by a reporter's capacity to understand. In the case of Emanuel Jaques there was thorough press coverage.

But what of the dynamics of the trial itself? Both the judge and the jury were expected to be cleansed of any direct knowledge of the Emanuel Jaques murder. Indeed, the jury was cloistered, or sequestered, during the entire trial. The members of the jury, who alone were to determine the facts, took no active role in the trial. They received only what the Crown and the defence presented under rules administered by the judge. If either the Crown or the defence had superior skills, the balance could have been tilted in their favour. This event which some call a morality play becomes a civilized form of trial by combat known and praised by the bar as the adversary system.

In the trial of Emanuel Jaques the public knew there would be conflict. If the accused could not afford counsel, they would be provided with such talent at the expense of the state. What the public probably could not perceive is that trial by combat would result in anything other than their perception of justice. They were soon to learn otherwise.

What were these rules of law? Wasn't this a simple matter? Weren't the lawyers and the judge there only to assist in presenting facts to the jury so that a verdict might be rendered? For an event to be a morality play the issue must not be complicated. The drama must be pointed and well defined. Can this be said of the Emanuel Jaques murder trial or, for that matter, any other trial? To help answer these questions consider one of the accused, Saul David Betesh.

There was a preliminary question as to whether Betesh was fit to stand trial. A question arose concerning his sanity. It was not for the jury to set the legal standard as to sanity. That had been determined long ago during the reign of Queen Victoria by judges and then reduced to written law. Under the criminal law if Betesh understood the nature and quality of his act (the murder of Emanuel Jaques), and if he knew the difference between right and wrong, then he was sane and responsible in law. He would have to stand trial for murder. If he did not understand, if he did not know the difference between right and wrong, then he would not have been tried. Rather, he would have been committed to a psychiatric institution.

The answer given by the examining psychiatrists was affirmative: under the criminal law, Betesh was fit to stand trial. But for some of the psychiatrists, the law made little or no sense. The law did not seem to address itself to the real issue of Betesh's sanity. The law did not seem to consider the history of a man who had found sexual ecstasy in raping, torturing, and drowning twelve-year-old Emanuel; who had a history of forcing boys as young as seven years old into painful sexual acts; who had pushed his mother down the stairs, thrown knives at his sister, and set a neighbour's home on fire as a child.

Betesh, along with the other defendants, was to stand trial. For four weeks and three days, eleven jurors heard the case against the accused. They lived sequestered in a downtown Toronto hotel away from their families. They were the instrument to test the guilt or innocence of those charged with the crime. They listened to the evidence following procedures more than seven centuries old, and they rendered their verdict on behalf of the community. Their role was not to judge the law, but rather to determine the facts under the law — nothing else. For some, including the police, their judgment was frustrating.

One of the four was acquitted, left to go free. One was found guilty of second degree murder, and two others, including Betesh, of first degree murder.

Bitter homicide detectives attacked the Crown attorney for "blowing the trial." To the police, the defendant who was acquitted was deeply involved in the murder. They could not understand a justice system that would let him free. They could not understand how defence counsel could assist in obtaining such freedom.

Nor for that matter could the father of Emanuel: "I just can't believe that this man is innocent. He must have heard the screams of my son. Why didn't he try to stop them? Why didn't he offer to help? And then he ran with the others." After his son was murdered the first reaction of Emanuel's father was to take his family back to their native Portugal, to the Azores, where he had lived on a small rented farm before coming to Canada. But he decided against the move because, "despite the tragedy, their future is in Canada."

In a very real sense, despite the anger of homicide detectives and despite the hurt of Emanuel's father, the fact is the criminal justice system worked reasonably well: it brought those charged with the death of Emanuel to trial and judgment. The public was made aware of the proceedings through the press. Yet can it be truly said that a moral judgment was made?

Betesh, for example, was twenty-seven years old when he was tried and convicted of the murder of Emanuel. He was given the mandatory life term. In law this means that in either fifteen or twenty-five years Betesh, then in his fifties, may be turned loose from prison — where he need not receive as a matter of right any psychiatric treatment. Indeed, the probability is that Betesh will be placed in isolation for the entirety of his sentence to protect him from the violence of other prisoners.

Did the public understand what can happen in fifteen to twenty-five years? Did they know that Betesh, untreated, might be freed? What end was achieved through this particular working of the criminal law?

All that can be said with certainty concerning the trial is that some testimony was reported in the press. There was keen public interest, and the jury deliberated carefully before reaching verdicts. It would be too much to call the trial a morality play for the community. There was too much that went unexplained. For the public to join in the moral judgment there must be understanding. At the present time that understanding resides exclusively with the members of the bar, that is, with the lawyers and the judges.

Still, the trial of those charged with the murder of Emanuel Jaques should be seen as the criminal law at its best. In less than a year following the murder, the accused were arrested, tried, and sentenced. There were no short-cuts; there was no undue delay; from beginning to end the public was informed. Those charged with the administration of justice in the trial relating to the murder of Emanuel Jaques had reason to be proud. They know only too well just how most criminal cases are handled.

Bargain Basement Justice

Only in slightly more than half of all reported crimes is there an arrest. And where an arrest takes place, charges are often dismissed long before a jury is assembled (assuming that a jury trial is permitted). The average criminal trial lasts for about eleven minutes, not for the month given over to the Emanuel Jaques murder case.

The reality of the criminal justice system has very little to do with a well-reported formal trial. It has much more to do with bargain basement justice as Crown attorneys, defence lawyers, and judges strain simply to handle the volume of cases that clog the court calendar. This is what the Law Reform Commission of Canada said of the criminal justice system:

Supposedly it [the criminal justice system] is a system designed to try defendants, assess their criminal liability on the evidence and determine the proper penalty in the light of all the circumstances; in real life trials are a comparative rarity. The vast majority of defendants plead guilty and the real work of the system takes place behind closed doors, between the crown attorney and the defendant's lawyer at the plea-bargaining table. Theoretically we demonstrate our public disapproval of certain types of conduct; in practice all we do is process an interminable series of recurring cases along the dreary assembly line of dime-store justice. Judges, crown attorneys, defence lawyers, police and all concerned in the operation of the system grow daily more disillusioned and discouraged. Small wonder many think our criminal law a hollow mockery.

The present task of the criminal justice system is simply to handle the case load. Ontario in 1976 strained under a backlog of 25,000 criminal cases. Defendants had to wait up to six months just to receive a first hearing. Often they waited in jails unable to raise bond, even under a liberal bail reform law. They waited in cramped cells of old jails. They waited at a cost to government of about twenty-eight dollars each day.

Along with the criminal cases was a backlog of 300,000 traffic offences from Metropolitan Toronto alone. And let there be no doubt that the traffic offences are to be considered a real part of the criminal law. Annually nearly one and a half million fines are imposed in the name of the criminal law. One third of these are for traffic related offences. In some provincial prisons, including those in Ontario, about half of the inmates are there because they could not pay the imposed fine.

Ontario took no hard look at why the criminal justice system was over-loaded. The government, like most governments, simply responded to felt pressure. The solution was to appoint forty more judges. Let them decide; let them imprison or mete out fines. The fact that assembly line justice was being entrenched did not matter.

In some communities, however, local magistrates began to take a different view. They began to ask what purpose should be served by the court in handling literally thousands of traffic citations. To some of the local magistrates, who often were not lawyers, the purpose of the law was to prevent the offence from being repeated, or, put somewhat differently, to encourage safe driving. The accused often seemed willing to co-operate; they did not come to court with lawyers; they came and pleaded guilty.

Fines, as such, hardly seemed to have an effect on the quality of driving. They certainly did not pay the cost of traffic enforcement, which is as much as fifty dollars an hour just to maintain a police officer and cruiser on active duty.

DISCOUNT JUSTICE

The local magistrates gave those found guilty a choice: they could either pay the set fine, or they could attend a film presentation on safe driving. The film was shown next to the courtroom; it took about an hour to run together with a brief lecture by a police officer. The point of the sentence was not to punish but to rehabilitate. It wasn't much of an effort, but it was a start. It was a way of asking offending drivers to view themselves and understand that they are part of a larger community, that their driving has an effect on others.

It is a weak programme. Whether it has any effect on dangerous driving is questionable. Yet, in Canada today new answers must be found. It is not possible to continue imprisoning and fining the guilty on a massive scale. It is not possible because of the numbers involved, the cost imposed on government, and the results achieved from such sanctions.

In Canada today, on any one day, roughly one in every thousand residents is serving time in a penal institution — a total of 20,000 imprisoned adult offenders. (This does not include the thousands of youthful offenders who are also imprisoned.) Although statistics are inaccurate, it has been estimated that more than 75,000 persons are held each year either in federal penitentiaries, in provincial institutions or in municipal jails.

> Close to one half of the 4,000 persons sent to penitentiaries each year are serving sentences for having committed non-violent offences against property or the public order. Indeed, less than 20 per cent of offenders are imprisoned for committing acts of violence against the person. Statistics reveal similar results in respect of provincial institutions. . . . One out of every seven persons appearing in court for the first time and convicted of a non-violent offence against property was imprisoned. On a second conviction for a non-violent property offence almost 50 per cent of the offenders were imprisoned. In the light of this type of information we must ask, what do we hope to accomplish by using imprisonment?

Behind the non-violent property and driving offences are some common problems. Not the least of these is that of drugs, including alcohol. In 1978 Ontario Correctional Services Minister Frank Drea gave this startling statistic: nine out of every ten persons in provincial jails, about 5,400, are there for "alcohol-related offences." That is, drinking had a direct relationship to the crimes committed. Specific estimates vary, but the general fact remains unchallenged. Drugs, including alcohol, are a large part of the problem relating to crimes for which imprisonment follows. In 1976 the federal Justice Minister Ron Basford estimated that 70 per cent of crime in major Canadian cities is drug related.

The primary concern of the law has been to catch the offender and impose stiff penalties. For more than fifty years little has been done to enquire into the causes for the crime, recognize their relationship to the community as a whole, and treat the offender so that there might be healthy re-entry into the community.

Impaired driving offers a case in point. The law has changed dramatically from 1910 when most provinces required evidence of intent to drive recklessly before a driver could be held liable. Now drivers must yield to breathalyzer tests. If those tests show a given level of alcohol the driver is guilty of an offence. Intent, so long an important part of the criminal law, no longer has a role to play. The crime is simply having consumed more alcohol than the law permits and being in control of a motor vehicle.

The crime brings a penalty which includes fine and imprisonment. But what has been done to cope with the underlying problem?

Neither the government nor the community ask themselves the question. The problem is frustrating in the extreme to the Ontario Minister of Correctional Services, Frank Drea. His government in 1978 moved to allow more liquor service on Sundays and in resort areas. The Minister said: "I don't understand how we can be at this particular time liberalizing a liquor control act . . . when I know . . . that just by the passage of that act we are going to have a 10 per cent increase of the number of people coming into our prison system. I honestly don't know what society wants. . . . The paradox is that society wants easing of drinking laws, but wants crackdowns elsewhere. . . . Yet here we are in the Legislature of Ontario going to make it easier to get a drink. Society really has to start taking a look."

The Minister understands the relation between alcohol and crime. His answer — limiting the availability of alcohol — is not necessarily the correct one. But he has stated the problem and raised a question the community must answer. Problems relating to alcoholism will not be solved simply by designating certain kinds of conduct as criminal. Indeed, all that is being done is to further overload an already encumbered system. Problems relating to alcoholism must be faced by the entire community. This does not mean that the community should deny itself more liquor service. It does mean that the community must understand some of the social cost that such greater availability brings.

Consider how British Columbia now deals with a related drug problem. The use of heroin is unlawful; the penalties for such use can be extreme. Crimes against property to finance the drug habit as well as violence against persons can rise dramatically as use of the drug increases. In 1978 Vancouver police estimated that about 60 per cent of all crime was drug related; much of the drug use is heroin addiction.

Vancouver probably is the leading North American centre for the receipt of heroin from Asia. It is estimated that there are 10,000 heroin users in British Columbia, approximately 60 per cent of the Canadian total. The annual dollar value, the amount of money that changes hands to pay for the drug in British Columbia alone, is $255 million, making heroin the fifth largest industry by dollar volume.

Arrest, trial, and imprisonment have not ended heroin use in British Columbia. The problem is widespread. Government has dealt with the matter on a community-wide basis. Heroin users now face compulsory medical care paid for by the government. The initiative for obtaining such care may be taken by the police, the courts, a doctor, a hospital, the user's family, or even the user alone. There is no stigma attached; there need be no conviction recorded. An evaluation panel will determine whether compulsory care is required, and there exists a right of appeal. Treatment can be on an out-patient basis, but for "hard cases" a 150-bed hospital has been readied. After the initial detoxification the province has provided for patient surveillance. And, more importantly, the province has allocated a relatively large sum for vocational training to help restore the patient to the mainstream of the community.

There are those who oppose the compulsory treatment programme on civil liberties grounds. They may be correct. The central point, however, is that the province of British Columbia has acted to treat a problem, drug use, in a community context. It has not assigned the problem to the criminal law alone. It recognizes that problems such as heroin use do not go away by labelling them as unlawful.

A community approach, however, does not mean that a problem will automatically be resolved. Nor does it necessarily eliminate the punitive aspect. Persons are held against their will. Elements of the British Columbia heroin treatment programme are somewhat suspect. The legislation is not directed to the causes of addiction; it offers only treatment after the fact — forcible treatment if necessary. It may even be that the province enacted the programme as it did because the federal government, which constitutionally controls criminal law, would not. Still, the fact is that a community approach has been attempted; that is what stands as value.

The Law Reform Commission of Canada warns:

> This job — condemning crime — is not an end in itself. It is part of the
> larger aim of producing a society fit to live in. Such a society is less one
> where people are too frightened to commit crimes than one where
> people have too much respect for one another to commit them.
> Fostering this kind of personal respect is a major aim of parents,
> teachers, churches, and all other socializing agents. One such agent,

though far less important than the others, is the criminal law. In its own way the criminal law re-enforces lessons about our social values, instills respect for them and expresses disapproval for their violation. This — what some call "general deterrence" — is the moral, educative role of criminal law.

CHAPTER
TWO

A System
without Purpose

"Anyone familiar with the police stations, jails, and courts of some of our larger cities is keenly aware that accused persons caught up in the system are exposed to very little that involves either judgment or solemnity." **James Q. Wilson, Criminologist and Writer.**

An Assembly Line without Direction

Without the support of the community the criminal justice system simply will not work. That support cannot exist without information. Unless the community knows how the system is working, intelligent, critical support cannot be forthcoming. Today the community walks in fear bred in no small measure by false information flowing from a system that is both cluttered and fragmented.

The trial involving the death of Emanuel Jaques was well reported in the sense of extended news coverage. Few events have received as much newspaper space or television time. Yet what did the public learn of the underlying issues, the moral issues which should frame the criminal law? What was the standard that allowed Betesh to stand trial as a sane person? Did the law offer an explanation to Emanuel's father as to why another of the accused was acquitted? And finally, what information was given concerning the sentences meted out to the convicted? How can a life sentence allow for freedom at the end of twenty-five years?

In this model of the criminal law where was justice? What could the public understand of justice, of the role of law? The news stories conveyed well the sense of conflict between the Crown attorney and defence counsel. The public had to understand that gladiators were fighting. But is the quality of justice to be measured by the strength of gladiators? If so, then how can there be respect for the rule of law?

The fact is that the Emanuel Jaques trial was conducted in accord with well defined rules of law under standards that do bear a relationship to morality. The burden was on the press and the broadcasting media to explain those standards and how they were implemented. That is one reason for the general rule allowing open trials; the public does have a right to be informed.

The Emanuel Jaques trial should have offered an example of the criminal law at its best. It should have been a morality play deeply involving the community. It was, to say the least, no morality play. The public was not well informed because only a few people are knowledgeable in the ways of the criminal justice system. They do not include the reporters, whose level of understanding is only slightly above that of the public.

On still a broader basis the public remains uninformed. They do not know the facts of crime, and that lack of information is reflected in conflicting feelings as to what the law should be. There are calls for the return of capital punishment; the courts are called "lax." Yet the conviction rate for homicide is about 90 per cent. Surveys conducted in the 1970s have shown that 89 per cent of the citizenry consider crime a "serious problem" but less than 10 per cent "worry about personal safety . . . as a serious concern." Yet four out of every ten Canadians are afraid to walk alone at night within a mile of their homes. A study conducted in 1976 by Professor Dan Koenig of the University of Victoria, British Columbia, found that Canadians are gripped by an exaggerated fear of being murdered or mugged. Professor Koenig found that Canadians are ten times more likely to be killed in a car accident than by a murderer, and that for every Canadian who is slain, four commit suicide. In Ontario, and indeed in urban Toronto, the chance of being victim of violent crime — murder, attempted murder, manslaughter, wounding, robbery, rape, or assault — are about the same as winning a prize in any given draw in the Provincial lottery. One in 200 are winners in the lottery, and one in 186 are losers to violent crime each year. The statistics offer no "true" picture of crime; they can be given different interpretations.

About 1972 the rate of violent crime in Canada began to level out. Within a few years actual decreases could be noted in British Columbia. The number of persons charged with criminal offences in British Columbia in the first seven months of 1976 dropped 2.2 per cent from the same period in 1975.

Still, what do the statistics and the surveys mean? To some, the credit is due to more effective police enforcement coupled with tough prosecution and sentencing. To others the decrease has little to do with police or court enforcement of the law; it has much more to do with a population that is growing older. About 90 per cent of violent crimes are committed by the young, those between the ages of sixteen and twenty-eight. For many years, because of the "baby boom," much of the Canadian population was in that category. Now the children of yesterday are the young adults of today. It is quite possible that crime is decreasing simply because the young are growing older.

The statistics and the surveys give no clear answer. The community takes the measure of crime by what it observes. First there is the law itself. Each time the law is violated, a crime has occurred, which can be noted and counted. In this regard, there can be no ignorance of the law; Canadians are presumed to know it. Now consider the meaning of this logic, this measurement of crime. Canadians are presumed to know the 700 sections that constitute the Criminal Code. (Each section of that code is a separate offence.) Add to this the 20,000 offences on the books of the federal government, and another 20,000 offences punishable by fine or imprisonment by the provinces. Left uncounted are the thousands of laws on the books of the thousands of municipalities. In Ontario alone in a twelve-month period in 1977, the court system received more than four million charges — approximately two charges for every three residents of the province.

To handle these charges there are rules of procedure, rules of practice. They determine what evidence will be received, and how — the ways in which cases are presented and heard. It is not difficult to understand the problems of the press in covering the Emanuel Jaques murder case. There are eight hundred rules that guide this system of criminal justice. As a gloss on these rules there are seven hundred years of court decisions; they provide interpretation. In some instances that interpretation radically changes the literal meaning of a rule. For the unwary the rules can be traps; they mark no simple path for the development of the "truth"; they do not allow those affected simply to tell their story to a jury of peers and ask for judgment.

In any complex criminal case, lawyers are needed. If they are not gladiators, then they must be seen as guides, whose responsibility it is to know the law and make it work for the client.

Yet the system is an assembly line. Those who view the system from within know this; they understand its flaws, and they are upset and critical both of the system and those who challenge it. In one sense they have become a real life fulfillment of a comic notion: they are the workers on an assembly line out of control.

The line irresistibly pushes material at the worker at an ever increasing and impossible pace. The frantic worker tries desperately to complete each piece — having to work faster and faster, but still unable to keep up. When working faster fails, the worker takes work from the line, to be done later during the slowdown that never comes. Pulling his hair, screaming in disbelief, the worker slaps the work together by any means possible, or sends it down the line untouched. The worker is far too harried to worry about what wil happen "down the line," much less what the final product will be. It looks like a Charlie Chaplin sketch, but it is far from funny. In the comedy climax the worker stops the line or is buried under the volume. The criminal justice system cannot be stopped, but the community may well be buried under it.

In the criminal justice system the work goes on. But no matter how frantic the pace, how quickly a trial is run, a plea accepted or a case forgotten, the backlog grows. There is no time to view and improve the whole system. As one successful litigation lawyer said about the need for change, "It is good for after-dinner conversation, but has no bearing on the practice of law. We're too busy dealing with the way things are; we have our own cases to handle."

And they are busy. The dimensions of the problem are staggering. The criminal justice system is made of, deals with, produces and is run by, rules. Obviously, the more the rules, the more cluttered and complex the system, the more diffuse the focus, and the more confusing it all is to the offender, the victim, the witness and the community.

There are four million charges each year in a single province. These are widgets on the line of justice. The line cannot be stopped (the widgets are people, after all), but it can be and is slowed. A single case may take several years to creep the length of the process. The delay grates on a sense of "justice," but it is the only choice.

The theory is that a case may be "remanded" (which is supposed to mean held for further inquiry) if there is a good reason. A remand has come now to mean that the case is being pulled from the line. One study shows that less than one-fifth of all charges arising from offences against the Criminal Code proceed *without* remand. This does not mean they are going swiftly toward resolution, only that they have not been pulled. Almost half of the charges were remanded once or twice. Fully one-quarter were remanded three or more times. Some comfort can be taken in knowing that only one per cent of charges were remanded more than ten times. The wheels of justice not only turn slowly, they are cracking under the load.

The delays might be acceptable if every person and every charge were fully heard. But this does not happen. Arthur Maloney, a prominent criminal trial lawyer who served as the Ontario Ombudsman from 1972 to 1978, described the problem of the provincial courts, where 90 per cent of criminal cases are tried. He noted that the purpose of the court is more than administrative efficiency. The court must also preserve the rights of the accused. These include due process of law, the notion of procedural fairness, and the guarantees afforded by the Canadian Bill of Rights.

Such are the concerns, but what is the reality of the process? Mr.

DISCOUNT JUSTICE

Maloney referred to the survey, undertaken in 1973 by the Canadian Civil Liberties Education Trust, of the courts in five major Canadian cities. It found that the provincial courts faced a daily average of more than twenty-five accused persons against whom there was an average total of almost forty-five charges. Only *eleven minutes* were spent on each case.

As a defence lawyer, it is not surprising Mr. Maloney stressed the danger to the defendant. But it must be noted that the court system and the community it serves also suffer from a need for speed. How great then is the moral force of such a "hurry up and wait" system?

Mr. Maloney continued: "One of the reasons that such stresses are created in the provincial courts is the ever-increasing number of offences over which they are given absolute jurisdiction. For example, theft under fifty dollars was under the absolute jurisdiction of a magistrate for many years, but it has recently been increased to theft under two hundred dollars. The reason for this no doubt was that those who draft the laws felt that the expense to the public of a jury trial was not warranted where the value of the goods involved [was so low]."

The jury trial was seen as a luxury to be done away with in the name of speed. The courts are jammed and the cases must be handled. The summary procedure by the magistrate, with a plea of guilty expected, was thought necessary. How could it be otherwise? In 1976 there were 195,516 reported thefts involving amounts of less than two hundred dollars! In that same period there were 37,524 thefts involving amounts of more than two hundred dollars. The courts, quite simply, cannot afford to give a greater amount of time to the charges.

Citizens are not expected to use the law in their defense. A retired high school teacher told this story:

> For thirty-two years I taught courses in my high school dealing with law. My students were told that the law was to be respected by all. This included not only the students, but also adults, police and the courts.
>
> One day a student received a ticket for going through a stop sign near the school. He asked to see a copy of the law relating to such signs. I gave him a copy. He read the law carefully. He found that for such signs to be erected there first had to be notice to the public, and there then had to be approval by the town council. He spoke with the town clerk and discovered that there had neither been notice nor approval by the town council. He appeared in court, presented his case to the judge. The charge was dismissed.
>
> What followed was little short of amazing. The chief of police himself came to the school. He demanded to know what right we had to teach such things to young people. He wasn't satisfied with the answer. Both he and the mayor wrote to our board of education. They asked that law be removed from the curriculum. Its teaching encouraged irresponsibility.

Here was a student who took his teacher's words to heart. He demanded to be treated fairly under the law. He interfered with the production line. To the chief of police and the mayor the danger was that others might do the same. Their view of the matter was that citizens should submit without question.

For the community to really know the law, and to use that knowledge fully, would sabotage the system of criminal justice. It would bring the assembly-line to a stand-still. What then is the purpose of the criminal justice system? According to the United States National Commission on the Prevention of Violence:

> A system implies some unity of purpose and organized inter-relationship among component parts. In the typical jurisdiction, no such relationship exists. There is, instead a reasonably well-defined criminal process, a continuum through which the accused offender may pass: from the hands of the police, to the jurisdiction of the courts, behind the walls of a prison, then back on the street. The inefficiency, fallout and failure of purpose during the process is notorious.

Save for maintaining the production line there is no unity of purpose in the criminal justice system of Canada. There is no certain punishment for infractions of the law. The purpose of the criminal justice system should not be to expose would-be criminals to a lottery in which they either win or lose, but to expose them to the solemn condemnation of the community if they yield to temptation. The criminologist and writer, James Q. Wilson, adds: "Anyone familiar with the police stations, jails, and courts of some of our larger cities is keenly aware that accused persons caught up in the system are exposed to very little that involves either judgment or solemnity. They are instead processed through a bureaucratic maze in which a bargain is offered and a hassle ensues at every turn — over amount of bail, degree of the charged offence and the nature of the plea."

This lottery especially penalizes first offenders and those guilty of minor crimes. They tend to plead guilty and to be processed quickly from plea to prison. They form the largest part of the group about whom Mr. Maloney spoke; from plea to sentence they often are heard in eleven minutes for each case.

Hardened criminals, those charged with systematic acts of violence, those savvy in the ways of the criminal law, will resist pleas of guilty. They will bargain over the amount of bail, the degree of the offence and the nature of the plea. Their most effective weapon is simply their willingness to fight. The Crown attorney does not have time for conflict through trial, except in unusual cases such as that of Emanuel Jaques. Anyone who threatens a fight impedes the flow of the production line.

The bargaining itself depends on the skill of counsel and the information available to them. Sometimes bad bargains are made by either the Crown or the defence. Sometimes the court is reluctant to accept the proposed bargain.

One senior Crown attorney put the matter this way:

> There is no doubt that criminal cases do get settled. It goes on all the time. If we fought out every case on our list we'd be twenty thousand cases behind. As the case load gets higher and higher there is more and more pressure to settle cases. In the magistrates' court, I'd say that twenty per cent are settled. We'd be willing to settle more of them, but defence counsel are unable to convince their clients to plead guilty to anything. As you get higher it would be about the same. In the Supreme Court assizes there were sixteen or seventeen cases. One was a pretty good case of capital murder but there were pitfalls in the case for the Crown witnesses and the two accused had been drinking. The prosecution accepted a plea to non-capital murder. The prosecution was delighted and the accused were delighted. There was also a rape case. It was a crummy case and the defence lawyer could probably have walked away with nothing but somebody told him to plead guilty to indecent assault and he did that. There was also a criminal negligence case which looked barely like dangerous driving. The defence was happy to get rid of the criminal negligence and wanted to plead to dangerous driving and I was delighted to accept that. Even with a plea of guilty to dangerous driving I had to strain to convince the trial judge that it was a case for conviction for dangerous driving. So there you are. Three cases settled at that level.

The Victim: Left in the Cold

This is an assembly line created without purpose. It processes the accused. It often does not even touch some perpetrators of both minor and major crimes. And, perhaps more importantly, *the criminal justice system moves without regard for victims.* Except as witnesses, victims play no central role in arrest, prosecution, trial, or sentencing. Yet it is the victim who has been injured. It is the victim who wants vindication and retribution. Margery Fry, an English penologist, stated: "The victim feels nobody cares about his stolen car or frightening experience because in law nobody does and nobody is therefore given the task of attending to his specific needs."

Consider the case of seventy-year-old Harold Hilton. A pensioner, he wanted to buy land for a retirement home. As a result of seductive advertising, he spent $6,580 for land near Kirkland Lake. After purchase he found that the land so glowingly described in the company's advertising was, in fact, an old mining site which was totally useless for his purposes.

Mr. Hilton started the process of suing the company for damages but dropped the case when the federal government began criminal prosecution under the false and misleading advertising section of the Combines Investigation Act. The government was successful. The company was fined a total of $30,000. On appeal, the fine was reduced to $21,000. The fine was lowered because, while the crimes were "particularly offensive," the judge said he could not "imagine that this is by far the worst case of misleading advertising in Canada."

But what of Mr. Hilton and his loss? *He will receive none of this money.* The appeal court judge expressed sympathy for Mr. and Mrs. Hilton, who had lost virtually all of their life's savings in buying land that "turned out to be totally unsuitable for building their retirement home." The court could do nothing to compensate them.

"If I had the authority to do so," the judge said in his decision, "I would require the appellant [the real estate company] to take back the property from Mr. Hilton [and] refund him the $3,680 purchase price, plus $2,900 that he expended in surveys and legal fees. Unfortunately, I have no such power."

This is not to say that Mr. Hilton cannot pursue a remedy. He can restart a civil action and sue the company. In fact the record of the federal government's case can be used to verify his claim. But he would have to go through a second procedure. He would have to spend money for lawyers and court costs. This is not easy for a pensioner who is trying to get back money he had saved. The very crime against Mr. Hilton makes it difficult for him to get satisfaction. It hardly makes sense. Two cases, rather than one, must be brought to aid the victim.

Mr. Hilton is unsure if he will sue. It was reported that he "has not made up his mind, because the experience has left him with a distrust of the law and lawyers."

And what effect does this case have on the offending company? It was caught and fined. Will the conviction deter? The total fine was reduced to $21,000. Yet the documents seized for trial showed that land purchased in 1974 for $64,000 was sold for $305,000. Even allowing for expenses and court fines, the arrangement remains profitable — despite the criminal conviction. It can be said that crimes of this sort do pay. Now this company, which appears to have large resources, may be squared off against Mr. Hilton, whose few resources were sunk into "almost useless" property. The company can use a great deal of leverage to ensure that if Mr. Hilton wishes to start a legal action, it can offer a "settlement" which will be accepted.

Mr. Hilton is a victim. He was a victim of false advertising — not only about the land, but about the criminal justice system. How much more satisfactory to Mr. Hilton, the system, and the community would the result have been if the courts were free to compensate the victim.

And, it should be added as Margery Fry did, "to the offender's pocket, it makes no difference whether what he has to pay is a fine, costs or compensation. *But to his understanding of justice it makes a great deal of difference.*"

Mr. Hilton is not alone. Most victims of crime not only are subject to the random, directionless flow of the assembly line, but they are also effectively left without compensation. Consider the case of Saul's Business Machines. In the regular course of business Saul's Business Machines rented photo-copiers to another company which, it was later found, had engaged in a large fraud operation. The police raided the premises of the company and seized equipment as well as records. Three months after the police raid, Saul's Business Machines was still waiting for the return of its photo-copying machines which had a value of about $3,000. There was no choice but to wait. There is no effective remedy against the government, and there is not even the barest hint that Saul's Business Machines was involved in the fraud. Moreover, it is likely that the machines will remain with the police, then be transferred to the Crown attorney for use as possible evidence. It is also likely that the owner of Saul's Business Machines will be called as a witness. He will be required to appear even if his testimony is not taken. For each day of appearance he will receive about $6.00 plus $1.50 in travelling money. No one will compensate him for the loss of business.

There are other, similar stories. A thirty-two-year-old mother of two found herself staring down the barrel of a gun when her grocery store was robbed of $240. She called the police; she expected help. This is what she says: "From the time I called the police on I was treated with no consideration, no feeling. . . . It isn't fair that criminals get all the rights and protection." Over a period of several months she appeared six times at police stations, preliminary hearings, and criminal court. She paid another person to run her store, at a cost to her of $300. For being a witness she received the same amount of money as the owner of Saul's Business Machines, $6.00 for each day of court appearance and $1.50 to travel between her business and the court.

In the end, the accused was acquitted. The evidence was simply the victim's word against that of the person charged. Now the store owner is out of pocket her loss from the robbery and the time spent assisting police and courts. In speaking to the press about her feelings she asked that her name not be used. She fears retaliation by friends of the accused. She is a person angry and afraid precisely because she acted as a good citizen and involved herself in the criminal justice system.

Mr. Justice Edson Haines of the Ontario Supreme Court warns: "There will come a time when witnesses no longer are ready and willing to appear to aid courts and the carrying out of justice. . . . Witnesses often realize that they are involved in an antiquated system that surrounds criminals with rights and protections and gives none to them. . . . It is unfortunate that while there are many powers existing over the witness (such as the power to compel presence at court) there are very few for him, for his protection, convenience and education."

The victim was not always hurt by the state. In Anglo-Saxon England there was no criminal law as it is known today. Disputes, wrongful acts, were settled between the parties or, if necessary, taken before a court where restitution was the order of the day. Punishments, including imprisonment, were rarely used. The courts more closely resembled those of our civil rather than criminal law.

Why then did the criminal law develop apart from the civil law? Why was the victim placed at such a disadvantage? After all, isn't the legal wrong that of injuring the victim?

Not so. The law declares that it is the state that is wronged, rather than the victim. Wrong was done to the state not Mr. Hilton, not Saul's Business Machines, not the thirty-two-year-old shopkeeper. Explaining the legal fiction which separates the victim from the accused and the wrong is no easy matter. One scholar wrote:

> As the common law developed, criminal law became a distinct branch of law. Numerous antisocial acts were seen to be offences against the state, or crimes, rather than personal wrongs, or torts. This tendency to characterize some wrongs as crimes was encouraged by the practice under which the lands and property of convicted persons were forfeited to the king or feudal lord; fines, as well, became payable to feudal lords and not to the victim. The natural practice of compensating the victim - or his relatives was discouraged by making it an offence to conceal the commission of a felony or convert the crime into a source of profit. In time, fines and property that would have gone in satisfaction of the victim's claims were diverted to the state. Compounding an offence [that is, accepting an economic benefit in satisfaction of the wrong done without the consent of the court or in a manner that is contrary to the public interest] still remains a crime under the Canadian Criminal Code and discourages private settlement or restitution. . . . It would now seem that historical developments, however well intentioned, effectively removed the victim from sentencing policy and obscured the view that crime was social conflict.

Cut through the words of legal scholarship and the answer that emerges is money. Quite simply, crime proved to be highly profitable for the state. If a crime were committed, if there were a victim of wrong, then the state might fine or confiscate the property of the criminal — not for the benefit of the victim, but for the coffers of the state. Crime and fines were a windfall to the Crown.

Has the theme changed over the centuries? Does the Crown today have any less interest in taking the money of the accused for wrong done? In the case of Mr. Hilton, exclusive of the cost of prosecution, the Crown profited from the wrong done to the tune of $21,000. Mr. Hilton received nothing.

Mr. Hilton is no unusual case. Money flows with great regularity from the pocket of the criminal to the treasury of the Crown with little for the accused.

Crime and Profit to the State

Legal scholars and judges know how the state profits from crime. This is what Mr. Justice A. M. Linden of the Ontario Supreme Court (then a professor of law) wrote:

> There is a great deal of money collected annually in Canada in the form of penal fines. In 1968, in Canada, 10,558 persons found guilty of their first indictable offences were given the option of paying a fine. Many more were so treated in summary conviction offences. In Ontario alone, in 1972, $31,314,795.84 were collected by the provincial courts (criminal division).
>
> Fines collected from offenders should not go to the state. They should go to the victims of the offenders. Preferably, individual offenders should be made to pay restitution to their own victims. . . . However, if there is no victim or if there has been no loss caused by the criminal conduct, the fine should preferably be placed into a fund for the benefit of other victims of crime. In this way, the criminal acts, the monetary penalties imposed for them and the victims' losses could be related to one another. Those who received compensation would realize that some of the money came from fines paid by various offenders. Victims would be more impressed by the humanity of the criminal law if the money collected were not confiscated by the state, but rather was paid to those who suffered as a result of the conduct. In imposing fines, judges would consider the fact that amounts levied would be paid to victims and would act accordingly.

The Kings of England knew what they were about. Fines and the confiscation of property were sure ways of raising funds without conflict. The accused were not in a position to complain. There was an understandable, though not particularly praiseworthy, policy behind the actions of the Crown.

The same cannot be said of modern Canada. The policy of the government relating to fines, like so many other aspects of the criminal justice system, lacks direction. Almost half of the prisoners in some provincial institutions are there because they could not pay the fines imposed. Yet it is costing the government more to maintain them than the amount of their individual fines. On balance, the cost of keeping a prisoner in a provincial institution for a year is about $14,000.

Individual fines involve amounts far less. What is more important, offenders often are imprisoned after they have made an attempt in good faith to pay what the courts have levied.

Who are the people imprisoned for non-payment of fines? They are poor, dispossessed, often native people. Not infrequently their crimes are alcohol-related and involve offences against property. Indeed, more than 60 per cent of the fines handed down were for amounts of seventy-five dollars or less. Yet these are the people being sent to provincial correctional institutions at a cost of $14,000 a year, or to local jails at a cost of about twenty-eight dollars a day.

In one study, 40 per cent of people imprisoned for not paying fines were found to have made partial payment either before being imprisoned or while in custody.

> This figure demonstrates a willingness but inability on the part of these people to pay the full amount of the fine which may also have been the case for some of those imprisoned who made no payment at all. Furthermore, several studies indicate that the types of offences for which persons are imprisoned for non-payment of fines are typically "poor people's" offences, such as vagrancy and drunkenness. In other words, the alternative jail term seems to fall discriminatorily on the poor offender. The discriminatory effect of the alternative jail term has been found in several provinces to weigh most heavily on the relatively poorer Indian population. In 1970-71 in Saskatchewan correctional centres 48.2 per cent of admissions were for non-payment of fines. However, 57.7 per cent of native admissions were for default of fines as compared to 34.7 per cent of non-native admissions.

Through absurd, random development the criminal justice system manages to hurt all those with whom it has contact. Too often, the victim is twice victimized. Whatever the accused might have taken, the state will be sure to add to the loss. There will be no real compensation for time spent waiting in a strange and hostile environment to testify before a court. Nor will there be compensation for the emotional drain as hostile lawyers pick away with none to safeguard the witness.

For the accused unlucky enough to be arrested and charged, the criminal justice system must seem like a lottery where chance, rather than reason, controls the result. The odds stand in favour of the criminal escaping arrest if the offence is minor and directed against property. But, if the person is once charged, the odds against him increase. New rules are set: if the accused has money, there will be freedom; if the accused is without money, there will be imprisonment. The reason? The judge who spins the wheel generally will make the chance of freedom dependent on the ability of the accused to pay a fine.

The fine may not be large. Still, it will be large enough for the poor to lose in the spin of the wheel. And once the poor have lost, that will be the end of the matter. Jail awaits. Neither the state nor the court will afford the accused the opportunity to work and pay the amount owing. The criminal courts do not like to see themselves as collection agencies.

It does not matter that the state will pay far more to jail the accused than is represented by the amount he owes. Nor does it seem to matter that jail tends to re-enforce crime, so that the pattern of continued petty offences becomes fixed.

There are alternatives to this self-defeating system. In itself there is nothing wrong with a fine as an alternative to jail. But what sense is there in levying a fine that cannot be paid? And, in any event, how much better it is to allow a person an opportunity to earn the money for payment than to imprison him because of his lack of immediate funds.

Why should the fines go to the state? The concern of the state is to prevent crime and to aid the victims of crime. Why shouldn't the revenue from fines be used to aid those who have been injured in their person or their property? It has been estimated that the total personal loss of property in Canada as a result of crime is about $40 million annually. Ontario alone in a single year received more than $31 million in fines imposed by the criminal courts. That sum is almost enough to provide full restitution to all Canadian victims of crimes against property.

Basic reform of the criminal law is not impossible. Yet this much is clear: the system will not change itself. Left alone, it will become more convoluted, more absurd. Reform does not require as a first condition the skill of experts. The people of the community can make judgments using their own common sense. Indeed, in no small measure the problems of the criminal justice system flow from the community's removing itself and allowing the priesthood of experts, with their mysterious rules which only they can understand and interpret, to assume control. The result is that under the sheer weight of the volume of rules and statistics the community, including the legislature, today does not even know fully the nature of crime or the effectiveness of the criminal justice system.

CHAPTER
THREE

The Victim
Alone

*Isn't it time for the state to ensure representation for the victim
as well as the accused?*

The Victim and the Courts

Too often the victim is alone. The criminal justice system, from police
to courts, treat the crime and not the victim's needs. The system does
what the law requires, but the price paid by the community and the
victim is high.

Dr. Justin Ciale points to the increase of armed robbery in Quebec
until 1971. Public frustration heightened. The criminal justice system
did not seem able to stop or even deter the violence of armed robbery.

Then, in 1970, the police took matters into their own hands.
Orders apparently went out to shoot to kill or wound if necessary. And
in that year at least a hundred offenders were shot. By January, 1970,
there were about 150 armed robberies. For the corresponding period in
1971 the figure was reduced by about a third. According to Dr. Ciale,
though it was regrettable, "most of the chaps were either killed or
wounded."

The police in Quebec seem to have geared themselves to a war, and
in such a conflict the courts of justice had only a small role to play.

The courts are an instrument of law. They are a free society's
alternative to the rule of the gun. But the rule of law must work in the
interests of the community. If courts do not concern themselves with
the victim, another response, one less civilized and far more brutal, can
be substituted. Capturing and imprisoning the offender will not in
itself restore money lost, or remedy the physical or emotional pain felt
by the victims of violent crime.

DISCOUNT JUSTICE

In 1973 there came before the British Columbia Court of Appeal for consideration an offence of the sort with which the police are familiar. A man with a lengthy record of violent assaults on others hurt a man and a woman. He was charged and convicted. The trial judge fined him $250 or, should he fail to pay, forty-five days' imprisonment. In addition, the judge placed him on probation for one year, a condition of which was an obligation to pay to the two injured victims $500 each.

An appeal was taken by defence counsel. There was no challenge to the fine. Indeed, the appeal court said the amount imposed was "lenient." The appeal questioned the power of the trial judge to order compensation to the victims. The appeal court solemnly reminded the trial judge "that it is most important that the sanctions of the criminal law and its administration should not be used, or be permitted to be used, for the purpose of enforcing civil obligations." The trial court was expected to enter a lengthy hearing on the ability of the offender's present ability to pay, and the precise nature of the victims' injuries. In the result, the appelate court struck the requirement of victim compensation.

The Crown collected $250 without the least question. The victims received nothing.

There was indeed a civil remedy for the victims of the assault. They could have sued the offender for damages. The criminal case would have had no special role to play in the litigation. The power of the criminal court and the moral sanction which should flow from it would have had no application. The likelihood of the victims' starting such a suit with its attendant costs was remote.

The legal right of civil litigation for victims of crime is usually only an empty shell. The civil law only appears to provide assistance; it rarely does so in real life. In one of the few studies on this subject ever done, the Osgoode Hall Law School surveyed victims of crime to determine how many victims actually brought actions against their attackers for wrong done. The results were little short of astounding: a total of 1.8 per cent collected anything from their attackers through litigation.

The study director stated:

> In other words, only three individuals out of 167 people interviewed received any financial reimbursement through tort law [the law of negligence]. Not only was tort recovery rare, but very few victims even considered suing. Fewer consulted a lawyer about their legal rights and still fewer actually commenced action against their assailants. Only 14.9 per cent of [those responding to the study survey] considered suing. Only 5.4 per cent consulted a lawyer, and only 4.8 per cent actually tried to collect something from their attackers. A study done

in British Columbia by Burns and Ross closely resembled these data.

The reasons for this dreadful recovery pattern were varied. Most commonly, victims expressed the view that it was not worth bothering to sue because the amount of their financial loss was small. Frequently, the identity of their attacker was unknown, or, if known to the victim, the offender would be unable to pay any court judgment against him. Some respondents were worried about the expense of launching a civil action. Others were concerned that the offender might attack them again, if they commenced litigation against them. Many of [those responding to the survey study] were totally unaware that they had any private legal rights. A few believed [wrongly] that their private legal rights were extinguished when the criminal action was begun. As a result, the [civil] system was of little avail in providing reparation to those injured by criminal conduct. It was primarily a paper right without much actual efficacy.

Some judges recognize the reality of the civil system. They understand that the criminal law should be concerned with the victim, and they have tried to bend the criminal law toward that end. They do not take the same narrow view as the British Columbia Court of Appeal. They also happen to be in the minority. On occasion, however, that minority speaks with great force. An Ontario High Court decision, for example, cited with approval a report of the Law Reform Commission of Canada: "Now that Her Majesty is no longer dependent upon fines in order to balance the budget, fresh consideration should be given to diversionary or settlement processes as an alternative to [the] disposition [of fine or jail]."

To see the importance of this alternative, consider the following example: Sam is a business man, forty years old, married, and living with his wife and two teen-aged children. He employed Sally in his shop for several months. More than once Sam made advances to Sally, and was rejected. On a winter evening in December all the employees except Sally had left the store. Sam locked the door and attacked her. She fought him, freed herself, and escaped. She went home at once and told her husband, who called the police. Sally had been bruised and her clothing ripped. Sam was charged with attempted rape, but in plea bargaining had the charge reduced to indecent assault.

This is what the court said in sentencing him:

Imprisonment would be of no assistance to the accused. It is likely it would ruin his one-man business. To him the conviction itself forms a substantial portion of the punishment. But in my opinion I must consider two other factors. This accused, as an employer, owed a duty to his female employees. If another employee or an intruder attacked a female employee, the employer would be expected to come to her defence. How much more must an employer restrain his own impulses for the protection of his female employees, especially where their duties often bring them in close physical proximity, often alone. Employers have a position of trust. They owe it to their employees and it is expected they will discharge it not only by the female employee herself but by the members of her family who permit them to work there in confidence.

There was a second factor that the court called even more important.

The victim. All too often she is ashamed, embarrassed and suffers in silence. Our system of justice spends substantial sums on the correction of the offender, and quite properly so. But what of the victim? She is left to her common law rights or a claim to the Criminal Injuries Compensation Board. Usually, she wants no more of the legal process and out of embarrassment declines to follow it, hoping to forget the nightmare of the event. Fortunately our criminal law has now developed to the point where the court is able to recognize her plight in some appropriate cases.

Then the court looked to the Criminal Code. It found provisions allowing it to order "restitution or reparation to any person aggrieved or injured by the commission of the offence for the actual loss or damage sustained by that person. . . ." The order can be made a condition of probation. And that is precisely what the court did. It placed Sam on probation for a period of three years, and made it a condition of his freedom that he pay $1000 to the victim.

The court did not force the victim to another tribunal. The court faced victim and offender. In the criminal hearing the very nature of the offence brought to the court full information as to the hurt inflicted on the victim. No further proof was required. In one hearing the court could pass upon the offence and bring a concrete remedy to the victim.

Was the case of Sally unusual? Did the personal and violent nature of the offence cause the court to stretch in order to find a remedy? If so, then the case has limited value. Most crimes do not involve violence. They are directed against property and the amounts are not large.

At about the same time that Sam's case was decided, the same court heard an appeal that does reflect the general run of criminal cases. Torek had broken into the home of Peter Kaminsky and taken a number of items. He was charged and found guilty of theft. The court imposed a prison sentence of just less than two years. (This allowed him to serve time in a provincial rather than a federal institution.) In addition, on the application of the Crown attorney, the court ordered Torek to pay Mr. Kaminsky $4,377.50. This represented the value, according to Mr. Kaminsky, of the goods stolen and never recovered.

The trial court did not make the order of restitution as part of an order of probation. It felt that the interest of the community required Torek to serve time in prison. It also felt that Torek should not be able to keep what he had stolen.

Torek appealed the order of restitution. He had been deprived, he argued, of many of the protections which he would have had in an ordinary civil action. There Mr. Kaminsky would have had to prove the value of his wife's ring instead of merely submitting a statement that it was worth $1,500. Mr. Kaminsky would have had to prove the amount of liquor which he claimed was taken as well as its value. In criminal court, Mr. Kaminsky had simply testified as to the quantity and value of the goods taken. Torek had been in no position to disprove.

If the trial had been in the civil courts Mr. Kaminsky would have been put to the burden of proving what had been stolen. Torek would have been without liability until Mr. Kaminsky carried his burden of proof. The role was reversed in the criminal case, and Torek claimed unfairness.

The appeal court recognized the difference between the burden placed on Mr. Kaminsky in proving the value of his goods in a civil as compared to a criminal trial. But it allowed the judgment of the trial court to stand. The appeal court stated: "It seems to me that it is a valid object in sentencing to prevent a convicted criminal from profiting from his crime by serving a jail term and then keeping the gains of his illegal venture." Torek, said the court, had had a chance to defend himself fully. The offence was theft and he had been found guilty.

With rare exceptions, however, judges do not concern themselves with restitution. Nor do Crown attorneys. Nor do the police. Mr. Justice Linden, then a professor of law, wrote:

> Restitution plays a minor role in Canadian criminal justice today. Primarily, it is used in theft, fraud, and malicious damage cases, where the accused appears able to repay the owner of the property he has taken or damaged. The full potential of restitution has never been achieved nor even seriously studied. Corrections officials have almost nothing to do with the problem, because virtually no one presently in prison is under any obligation to make restitution. Many of these prison authorities support the idea of restitution but they have no control at all over the sentencing function of the courts. . . . The victim is seldom aware of his rights. Occasionally, he may ask the police or the Crown for restitution or he may speak out in court. One Crown counsel told me of an incident where a complainant in an assault charge, during the sentencing, stood up in court waving his broken eyeglasses in the air. He took the hint, asked the court for restitution for the cost of the glasses and it was ordered by the court as a condition of probation.

The rarity of restitution as a condition of sentence or probation is reflected in statistics. In a survey of records covering over 4,294 convicted appearances from 1967 to 1972 restitution was ordered only for six convictions — .1 per cent of the sentences. Instead of being an active force in bringing offender and victim together, the statistics make it clear that the criminal courts have forgotten the historical function of the criminal law. Now the courts, including judges, administrators, and Crown counsel, justify their inaction by arguing that the criminal courts should not become a debt collection agency for the victim.

The Victim and the Criminal Meet

It is not the state, nor any appendage of the state that is using the device of restitution. Rather, it is defence counsel. The obvious hope is that restitution to the victim may bring a reduced charge or a lighter sentence to the accused. Often the device of restitution works. Sometimes it does not, and when this happens the court, in effect, can abet the very crime for which the accused has been charged. The story is told of a travel agent who embezzled $50,000. His lawyers tried to convince him to make restitution. If he had done so, his sentence would have been about six months. He refused. The sentence given was eighteen months. In substance, the accused chose to keep the $50,000 and spend an extra year in jail. It probably was not a bad idea; he was unlikely to be able to earn $50,000 in a year. Yet can there be any doubt that the interest of the community and of the accused might have been better served if the court had required him to pay back the stolen money?

The court allowed the accused to reap the benefit of the embezzlement. Neither defence counsel nor the Crown raised the matter of restitution. The case is very much like that of Mr. Hilton, the victim of a land swindle. The wrongdoer is fined or imprisoned, and the victim gets nothing.

Who speaks for the victim? To the Crown, the victim is only a witness. To the defence, the victim is much like an adversary. To the court, the victim all too often is incidental to the crime and to the case of the accused. In the result, the victim usually gains little from the process, even assuming that it works effectively. The cases involving restitution or reparation are far from the norm.

The law could be otherwise. The fragments of law are there to pull together once more the string that connected the accused and the victim. A 1959 English White Paper entitled "Penal Practice in a Changing Society" stated: "It may well be that our penal system would not only provide a more effective deterrent to crime, but would also find a greater moral value, if the concept of personal reparation to the victim were added to the concepts of deterrence by punishment and reform by training. It is also possible to hold that the redemptive value of punishment to the individual offender would be greater if it were made to include a realization of the injury he had done to his victim as well as to the order of society, and the need to make personal reparation for that injury."

Restitution is more than money. It is a means for the state to say to the victim that it cares. More importantly, it is a way for the state to exert its power in aid of the victim — not to release the accused from responsibility, but, rather to charge the criminal with the burden of making right the wrong.

The matter can be put somewhat differently. Let the state be seen as a parent, and the accused as its child. A function of a parent is to help the child to grow to independence, to assume responsibility. Suppose a child destroys property belonging to a neighbour. A parent could provide compensation for the wrong done, and punish the child. Or a parent could take the child before the neighbour, point out the wrong, and demand that the child pay the damages. To take the second course is not easy. It requires the parent to spend time in the confrontation between the child and the neighbour. It requires the parent to help the child shape a programme to earn money and repay a portion of that earned. For a wealthy and busy parent the cheapest course is to repay the money and punish the child. To do this, however, is not to face the child personally and realistically with the damage done. It allows the child to make excuses, to believe, as many prisoners do, that either they were not guilty of any crime or that someone else, namely, the community, should be blamed for their actions.

Nor does the easy course help the injured neighbour. There is protection only so long as the parent will intervene. There is no assurance that the child will behave, that child will grow into a good neighbour, who not only will abstain from injuring others, but will assume the positive duties of a citizen.

Professor Stephen Schafer has put the matter well:

> To restore the injured victim to his pre-crime position is primarily the obligation of the offender. The offender should be required and permitted by the penal system to fulfill this obligation. Such an approach would further the interests of the victim, and also perform a rehabilitative function within the penal system. If the offender were permitted to be at liberty, either immediately following conviction or after a reduced sentence, on the condition that he use that opportunity to make restitution to the victim, penal rehabilitation goals would be furthered and society would be freed of the double burden of compensating the victim and providing penal shelter to the offender.

Restitution is compensation made by the criminal himself, ordered by the criminal court and accomplished by the offender's efforts as part of his criminal sentence. The compensatory aspects of restitution are no less justified than is compensation itself. Correctional restitution, however, offers more to a solution of the crime problem. It does not allow the offender to terminate his relationship with his victim, but rather forces this relationship to be maintained until the victim's original position is restored. This is what our modern understanding of the criminal-victim relationship demands. Correctional restitution is the type of compensation that holds the promise of both restitution to victims of crime and implementation of the reformative and corrective goals of the criminal law.

This so-called modern society has a long way to go before victim and accused can meet and come to an accommodation. The state, instead of leading the way, insulates the accused from the victim. The criminal has a choice, and the victim does not. The criminal gets medical attention, a lawyer paid for by the state if he cannot afford one, room and board and, when sentenced, opportunities to improve his education and job skills as well as possible assistance after release. By contrast, the victim pays his own bills, replaces his own property losses, misses work, and pays his own costs during trial proceedings. The victim winds up unsatisfied, and often in fear of retaliation.

The community imprisons the criminal at a cost ranging from $14,000 to $17,000 a year. Yet, while in the prison, the opportunity to earn a decent wage and repay the victim is largely denied him. Until quite recently, prisoners earned only about $3.00 to $4.50 *a week*. Reform has now brought those performing industrial work to the minimum wage.

Following an initiative taken by the New Zealand government in 1964, the provinces and the federal government of Canada have acted to compensate victims of crime. However, the policy behind that decision is unclear. It wavers between a scheme of compensation by government and one of restitution by the criminal. It smacks of a right and, at one and the same time, of welfare. Mr. Justice McRuer of Ontario stated in his 1968 Royal Commission on Civil Rights:

> As government becomes more and more committed to the concept of a welfare state with programs for state education, health services, and unemployment relief, no great philosophical revolution is required for the acceptance of the principle that, within limits, the innocent victim of crime should also be compensated or given relief by the state. . . .
> The state has undertaken to protect the individual from his aggressive neighbour, and when it fails to do so the victim of the aggressor should be compensated. It is suggested that by paying taxes to support police forces and other agencies of law enforcement, the public in a sense is financing an insurance scheme against crime, and consequently the

individual member of the public deserves reimbursement for losses due to crime.

The effect of the state's decision is that it, rather than the criminal, will be primarily liable for wrong done. The criminal is further insulated from the victim. For its part, the state will determine whether compensation will be paid, and the extent of the award. In the final analysis, the matter can become one of dollars rather than the rehabilitation of the victim.

Criminal injuries compensation boards have been established in the provinces to interpret and administer the law. Limitations have been imposed upon them that reflect the state's concern with money. They have been permitted only to compensate for acts of violence. They cannot pay for loss of property. Compensation would have been denied in the stories told about Mr. Hilton and those swindled by the travel agent. It does not matter that they suffered emotionally. Yet if a victim had been assaulted or raped compensation could be paid both for actual injury and for "pain and suffering," which includes the mental anguish following an attack.

Still another limitation has been imposed on criminal injuries compensation boards. They must pay only for actual injury. They must attempt to quantify, to put a precise dollar figure on the hurt. They must also determine if the victim has received money from any other source in payment for the wrong done. The tendency of these limitations is to treat the victim as a welfare case, rather than a citizen deserving help, including compensation.

Consider first the need to quantify the injury. The Ontario board was asked to award money for pain and suffering to a victim, who, in the words of the board "was beaten into insensibility, sustaining severe and permanent damage to the skull and brain, other organs and limbs and these devastating injuries have left him unable to speak, or perform normal functions and have largely deprived him of mental capacity." The board nevertheless denied any award for pain and suffering:

> There is no doubt that the claimant suffered pain and shock as the result of the beating he received, although he was beaten into insensibility, and would continue to suffer varying degrees of pain after regaining consciousness and during hospitalization. However, since leaving hospital and entering the nursing home his state has been one of euphoria. He has no realisation of loss due to mental incapacity resulting from his injuries. He is free from care, strain or worry since he quite clearly lacks the mind to encompass such things. Present responsibilities and obligations and future concerns would not appear to be within his ken and it seems quite evident that past events are

forgotten in so far as this incident is concerned, although he has recollection of his birthplace and former home. He is not depressed but cheerful and his mind is not saddened by any appreciation of loss of mentality or physical ability, simply because he has lost the mental capacity as a result of severe brain damage to realise his state and condition. . . . In short, he is not suffering so there is no continuing pain and suffering to be taken into account.

The more complete the criminal's work, the less the state will have to pay. Such seems to be the effect of the board's ruling.

Compensation boards, at times, seem required to take the worst of the common law and to disregard the best. The decision concerning pain and suffering, in its conclusion comes directly from the common law. The principle, however, has been lost in the pursuit of words. The principle is quite simple: at the time the wrong was inflicted surely the victim felt pain. Surely the victim suffered. Isn't that the test to determine compensation?

On the other hand, the common law would address itself exclusively to the wrong done. It would measure that wrong and demand that the wrongdoer pay. It would have no effect on the nature or size of the judgment if the victim had insurance or were paid under some other scheme for the hurt done. This is not the case under the law establishing compensation for victims of crime. The board will deduct from its award any amounts paid to the victim by, for example, workmen's compensation or welfare or private insurance. The result is that the compensation plan tends more and more to become a welfare rather than an insurance scheme. This inhibits victims from requesting compensation. They may feel, or others may feel, that what the board offers is charity.

Yet, viewed either as welfare or as insurance, the victim compensation programme is not costly. It is funded largely by the federal government and administered by the provinces under provincial law. Listen to the funding formula and judge the extent of government's commitment to the victim: financial support is available to provinces compensating victims of crime to the extent of the lesser of 90 per cent of the cost of the programme or *five cents per capita whichever is the lesser amount.*

Ontario is the most populous province. Yet in 1973-74 its criminal injuries compensation board paid out $722,637 to victims of crime. This was twenty times the amount paid in 1969-70. In 1973-74 the board received 510 applications for reimbursement, and heard 386 of them. From 1968 to 1970 the board received only 105 applications and heard 39 of them.

Now weigh the importance of the amount spent in 1973-74. The year before, in 1972, the province collected in the form of fines from its criminal courts more than $31 million. The federal government paid to the province 90 per cent of the cost of its victims of crime compensation programme or five cents per capita whichever is the lesser. At the very most, this meant that the province paid about $320,000 to victims of crime. It collected in the form of revenue from fines imposed by criminal courts almost a hundred times that amount.

The reality is that both the federal and provincial governments could be far more generous to victims of crime without the need to draw on general revenue funds. The monies are there in the form of fines imposed. It would have been possible for Ontario alone to have paid full compensation for almost all of the personal property lost to criminals in Canada as a whole — solely from the fines collected by Ontario criminal courts.

In Aid of the Victim: A Proposal

The limitations imposed by law on the criminal injuries compensation boards are great. Yet, even within these limits there is real potential to aid victims of crime. To illustrate and emphasize what can be done, consider the rape victim. The nature of the crime is particularly hurtful. And that hurt can be heightened by the trial. It often seems that the victim rather than the accused is on trial. The details of the crime are drawn before the public. Defence counsel does not stop here. There can be harsh probing into the sex life of the victim as the defence tries to prove consent to the act. For the victim the trial is generally an ordeal with no redeeming virtues.

Properly used, though, compensation law can meet many of the needs of the rape victim (as well as those of other victims of crime). The state, through its instrument, the criminal injuries compensation board, will decide whether a crime has been committed — whether, for example, the applicant for compensation has been raped. The offender is notified of the hearing and given an opportunity to "defend." If the board awards compensation, it has the power, in law, to recover the amount of that award from the offender. The board may, in addition, find that the applicant was raped, but that she *contributed* to the crime, that she was in fact somewhat responsible. In this regard, there is a wide difference in the legislation between Britain and the provinces of Canada. In Britain special provisos have been written into the law concerning sexual offences. An English author summarized his nation's approach to compensation to the rape victim:

> The intention to include sexual offences in any scheme for
> compensation always has given rise to considerable misgivings. It has
> been pointed out that there may be complicity or inducement by the
> victim. The girl who finds herself pregnant as a result of a seduction

may make an allegation of rape in order to attempt to protect her reputation, though the offence must be promptly reported to the police. Sexual offences by their very nature nearly always take place in private, away from actual or potential witnesses and are very difficult to establish convincingly. . . .

The board is required to scrutinise all sexual cases with particular care. In rape cases the awards appear to have been rather on the low side, probably because the board has been alive to the danger of abuse, and also because there are no precedents in civil cases for awards of damages for rape. A clear distinction appears to have been drawn between the wholly innocent victim of rape and the victim who was to some extent to blame.

Ontario, like most of the other provinces, does not hold to the British view. Rape is treated as other crimes. The victim is not singled out for disbelief. In point of fact, not a single victim charging rape in more than four years of reported Ontario experience has been denied compensation. *Not a single victim charging rape in more than four years of reported Ontario experience has had her claim lessened because of alleged responsibility for the crime.* This was explained by Ontario Chief Justice Bennett in 1971:

> The Board may decide that a crime was committed whether or not the offender was prosecuted or convicted. . . . This is so even where the offender was known but was not prosecuted or convicted. The burden of proving a criminal offence before us is less onerous than in a criminal court. *The standard of proof before us is, as indicated, on the balance of probabilities and not beyond a reasonable doubt.* Again, evidence is available to our Board which cannot be presented in a court of law. For instance, the offender may have given evidence at an inquest . . . which cannot be used against him in a subsequent criminal or civil proceeding, but is admissable before us. . . . And [in addition] hearsay evidence is admitted to some extent.

The rape victim comes before the board having first reported the crime to the police. That report is brought to the board for examination. The hearing itself may be closed to the public where the nature of the crime and the effect on the offender so requires. Further, the board may order the report of its award published in only summary form to protect the victim. Finally, the board, once it finds a crime committed and once it enters an award, may ask the attorney general to collect on the money paid. The state can move against the offender for the amount of the award; the action would be brought in the name of the state and the victim need not testify further. The state need only prove that on the *balance of probabilities* the offender committed the crime. The offender then will be liable for the amount of the award.

The rape victim is afforded vindication. (A crime has been committed and this has been so declared by the state.) The rape victim is afforded retribution. (The offender can be made to pay the amount of the award.) The rape victim is afforded redress. (The board can pay up to $15,000 in a lump sum payment, or $175,000 in periodic payments not exceeding $500 monthly.)

All of this can be done without the trauma of publicity or the tension and disorientation of the trial process. All of this can and is being done in Ontario and other provinces with a sense of humanity. The Ontario Criminal Injuries Compensation Board does more than pay actual medical expenses. It also compensates for loss of income, the inability to work resulting from the crime. More importantly, the board *will compensate* for "pain and suffering" which goes beyond actual provable damage. And in all of the reported rape cases before the board the larger portion of each award was for pain and suffering.

The board, as we noted before, has applied itself to the question of rape. Not a single claim of rape has been rejected. Not a single claim has been denied some compensation for pain and suffering. Nor, it must be emphasized, did the board require the offender be found guilty, or for that matter, found at all. The board heard the facts and rendered judgment.

Can there be any doubt that the work of the board serves the interest of the victim and the state? How little change is required to make the board *more* effective by integrating it into the functioning of the criminal justice system. Criminal courts could call upon the board to assist victims of crime and, at the same time, to order restitution by the accused. It would be the function of the board to ensure payment by the accused, but the board would have the support of the criminal court. Further, sentences could be imposed that would allow the accused the opportunity to work. A line of distinction can and should be drawn, between denying an accused his freedom in retribution for wrong done, and denying that person the right to earn a living. To effect the kind of change noted does not so much involve major changes in law as in attitude. Those agencies, courts, and administrators directing the criminal justice system must recognize that it is a single system designed to secure the state by assisting the victim as well as reforming the criminal. Isn't it time for the state to ensure representation for the victim as well as the accused?

CHAPTER FOUR

On the Front Line: The Police

"It's too bad the judges and those lawyers don't stick with us on the street for a while and see how long their funny language and fancy robes last." A police officer.

Street Corner Justice

The police share the frustration of the victim. To investigate a case, lay charges, prepare the Crown attorney and then see the matter dismissed or the charges reduced through "back room" plea bargaining, is hurtful. Too often the police feel demeaned, treated as incidental to the trial, and bruised in their sense of professionalism. One officer said:

> We feel like grade ten drop-outs with pea-sized brains . . . while those bigwig lawyers fly around in the Halloween robes and play their funny games. . . . Some of them make us look like perfect asses in court and then they [the criminals] get the same light sentence and they serve it in a joint that puts them to work on a garbage truck or something equally useful and they call that rehabilitation. . . . Mind you, if you get the right case in front of the judge that you know is going to be hard on the guy, then it is okay because he goes up for a stiff sentence. . . . It's too bad the judges and those lawyers don't stick with us on the street for a while and see how long their funny language and fancy robes last.

The police are both angry and confused. What is the sense in conducting an investigation and making an arrest if the case will not be prosecuted? What are the police to say to the victim? How will the offender react if he believes that charges laid can be set aside?

Said another investigating officer,

Sometimes we wonder what the thinking by the judges is, when they hand out sentences. It is obvious that they really have no idea of all the things that offender has been up to and the cops begin to get the feeling that the lawyers and the judges think that we lay out a charge without too much reason. If they thought that we knew a lot about the offender and might have been working on the investigation of all his activities for some time, maybe they would realize that we feel the guy really needs some form of help or detention. But the legal profession [in the courtroom] figure we are just doing our job and arresting everything that moves.

For the police officer there is a challenge: if he honestly believes that an offence has been committed, then how can a conviction be obtained? It is not enough to investigate and lay a charge. The police must bear in mind the reality of the criminal justice system. The police, in their own way, must become advocates. A young offender, along with four of his friends, was brought to court for the fifth time in a two-month period. The police saw him as a "bad egg." He was brought in on eight charges ranging from violation of the Narcotics Control Act to Criminal Code offences such as breaking and entering and assault. On the morning of his appearance the police made a deal. If the youth would plead guilty to theft, breaking and entering, and possession of narcotics, the other charges against him would be dropped and, more important, the charges against the youth's friends would be dismissed.

The police thought they had a deal, and that they had the better part of the bargain. The accused did as he promised. He pleaded guilty without representation by counsel. The court then remanded him for sentence. While he was being held, but before sentence, the police acted against his friends. They arrested them on other charges. The police thought they had made the system work for them. In the result, they were proved wrong, and, it can be said, everyone (except defence counsel) came out of the experience a loser.

When the young offender discovered that his friends were in custody, he obtained a lawyer, and changed his plea to not guilty. There followed a six-month delay and then a trial and sentence in county court. The accused was given fifteen months in a correctional institution. "The police were furious that the offender got a 'light sentence' in view of his record and their knowledge of his involvement in crime; the offender was completely negative to the entire process and felt he had 'been messed up' by the whole performance; the defence attorney was pleased that he had been able to 'get a satisfactory sentence'; and the Crown attorney, who had not been apprised of all the facts, was indignant to learn after disposition of the case, that there had been an agreement in the first instance between the policeman and the offender."

The police stand at the front line of the criminal justice system. They are both visible and vulnerable. The courts, the judges, the lawyers, and the correctional officers are more removed. For the police to serve and protect the community is no easy matter. And the job becomes especially difficult if there is a failure in the system. All too often the police take the brunt of criticism that is better directed toward others.

For example, in 1975 the Toronto Rape Crisis Centre fastened upon the police as a significant reason why many women rape victims did not report the offence, or if they did, felt keenly disturbed by the "justice" to which they had been subjected. Toronto Councilwoman Dorothy Thomas, speaking for the Rape Crisis Centre, called upon the police to investigate the complaint with the view toward establishing a special sex or rape squad.

In-depth interviews with 132 victims of rape, however, brought another response. The fact is that they had few complaints directed toward the police. (They preferred senior officers, whether male or female, to handle their charge from beginning to end.) Their complaints were strongly and directly aimed at the courts and the Crown attorney. This is what was said in a report that has too long remained confidential:

The survey team encountered harsh criticism of the court system by the complainants [victims of rape]. It became clear to the interviewers that all the victims who appeared in court were severely affected by the procedure. No matter what the disposition, the court was the part of their experience that most distressed them except for the rape itself.

1. All disliked the long period between the arrest of the rapist and the beginning of the trial and lengthy court proceedings.
2. Many had bitter complaints regarding student groups and other visitors in Court while they were giving evidence and being cross-examined.
3. Juveniles resented that their parents were not allowed in Court and parents resented the exclusion.
4. Many did not know the function of a Crown Attorney nor did they feel they had adequate consultation with him.
5. Some would prefer the Crown Attorney to use language that complainants could understand.
6. Some wondered why they had to deal with several Crown Attorneys during the prosecution.
7. Many did not understand the reasons for conviction or acquittal.
8. Many did not understand why they were not allowed to remain in the courtroom after they had completed their testimony.
9. Many resented what they considered to be vicious cross-examination, particularly that related to their sexual activities and their moral character.
10. Some surmised it would have been better to have their own lawyer to protect their rights.

Consider what the police must do if they want a rape charge to hold up in court. They know of the strong possibility that the Crown will bargain away a rape charge if the evidence is not substantial. They know that the defence is capable of taking the victim through tough cross-examination which can shatter the victim still suffering from the shock of a personal and brutal assault. They know that the elements of the crime itself must be proved. They are in no position to challenge the law; they must, for example, gather the facts which prove that the victim did not give her consent. They must, in sum, ask questions of the victim which are personal and can seem terribly hurtful. They must do all of this in the name of justice. What is surprising is that the police are held in such high regard bearing in mind the job that they must do.

A large part of police duty involves the exercise of discretion. The police have the power to effect many arrests. Indeed, it is safe to say that if the police ever worked "to rule," if they ever arrested all who violate the law, much of the community would be in jail. The power of the police in no small measure means the power that they chose not to use.

> At the time of confrontation or arrest you just play the thing by
> ear. . . . It depends on your mood, the suspect's attitude and actions,
> what the offence is. . . . There are so many things that play a part in the
> arrest . . . or non-arrest. . . . Hell, if a guy is just about to go off shift he
> may decide, if it is a minor thing, to let it go, instead of going through
> all that paperwork . . . like it's all unconscious as to how you go with a
> thing. . . . But after the fact you think of all the things that made you
> proceed the way you did. . . . You name a thousand things.

Arrest is the use of power; it is confrontation. It is not something that most police enjoy doing. They, like most of us, prefer a comfortable and pleasant kind of job, but they soon learn the ways of the street. Listen to the words of this police officer:

> There is no way people are going to think I'm a great guy, when I'm
> arresting people on warrants, nailing them for speeding and stuff that
> they have done against the law. . . . Hell, no one wants to be caught by
> the big, bad officer. . . . And a lot of guys [police officers] like to feel
> they have the upper hand at an occurrence and come on like Mr. Big . . .
> not necessarily rough, but with a lot of power. . . . I guess it is hard
> because the force makes you feel a lot of respect and I guess that we
> want to be respected and some guys figure the way to get respect is
> to act important.

The need to be respected is a constant in all police work. Some officers command that respect with more firmness than others. But the final use of power is in their hands. Government has given them both the gun and the club. In no small measure they are recruited and trained in terms of their capacity to use both. An officer may decide to ignore a violation of the law. Yet, if the wrongdoer talks back, if there is personal affront, the officer may use the power that exists.

A police officer asked a young man to identify himself. He did so but, in the words of the police:

> He started mouthing off, "You silly cops, you can't put me in jail," and acting smart. After that I went through active vagrancy file, and there was nothing on him. But I take a certain pride in my work, and I finally got him into jail. I had to do it on my own time, but I finally busted him for a burglary at a store. I caught him busting out with a carton of stuff from the store.
>
> I had a hunch he would hit the store. So each night I'd put on my plain clothes, and I'd wait in the dark, watching the place in the cold. The night I caught him I was about to leave. Boy, it was cold, when sure enough, he comes walking up the driveway with a couple of guys, carrying pry bars. Then they break the lock, and they're coming out with the carton. I get a gun on them and say, "Don't run fellas. If you do, I'll kill you. Just don't tempt me, or I'll have to shoot." After, I told him his mistake was calling me names. "You shouldn't talk to a policeman like that."

The police are not programmed machines. They are part of the community. They, too, have homes and families. For the most part, they come from a middle class background, and they carry a work ethic to their job. They, themselves, work hard for the pay received. They are not made wealthy by their work. They struggle to maintain their middle class status in the same way as other wage earners.

A Person for All Seasons: Job Definition

Yet society expects enormous qualities from these people of the community. Their job is probably far more complex than that of any other profession. On the one hand, "we expect our law enforcement officer to possess the nurturing, caretaking, sympathetic, empathizing, gentle characteristics of physician, nurse, teacher and social worker as that officer deals with school traffic, acute illness and injury, juvenile delinquency, suicidal threats and gestures, and missing persons. On the other hand, we expect this same officer to command respect, demonstrate courage, control hostile impulses and meet great physical hazards . . . control crowds, prevent riots, apprehend criminals, and chase after speeding vehicles." There are no other professions which demand such opposite characteristics, and, it must be added, pay so little.

The police are not physicians. They do not have the education or the training. They are not psychiatrists. Nor are they social workers. Yet, in a very real sense they perform all of these functions.

More than anything else the police are a social service organization. They do not function so much to prevent crime as to control difficulties, to ease trouble, whether it is a family dispute or snarled traffic. The bulk of police time is not spent tracking killers. The police stand as the only social service agency open twenty-four hours a day, seven days a week, 365 days a year. Doctors have their hours of work and their answering service. Social service agencies tend to close at 5 P.M. The police are always there.

There has been acceptance of this expanded role both by the community and the police. Many police forces are unionized. There have even been strikes called. To date, however, the police have never questioned their role as social service agency. Officer Abraham said to an interviewer:

> We aren't turning anything down. We're not a pick and choose agency, anyway. If Mrs. Smith phones and says her plumbing is on the fritz or her cat is up a tree or little Johnny phones us about his bike being stolen, well we're not going to say "Go away!" I mean we respond to all these calls. Just like a bank robbery. Mind you, we assess our priorities and go to the bank hold-up first. Because of this, the word's got around: phone the police, they don't turn you down.
>
> Another thing is that we are one of the few social agencies — if you want to accept that we are a social agency — that is open twenty-four hours a day as opposed to the usual nine to five, Monday to Friday, so we are available. And when somebody wants a psychiatrist at three o'clock in the morning and they call the hospital and they can't get a psychiatrist, who else are they going to turn to but the police car floating around? They know that we are always there for something.

The police are not prepared for their work by years of university education. Often they hold only a high school certificate. As cadets, their formal police education, their classroom experience, lasts for months rather than years. Their real education comes on the street, following senior officers, trying to understand how they are to conduct themselves in the context of department regulations and life experience.

> You never know what you are going to get thrown at you. . . . In one day you will get a call to a disturbance. . . . You get there and find some woman screaming at the husband and threatening to kill him and herself. . . . She is violent — one bad move and she'll go over . . . you gotta play shrink and Mr. Cool and at the same time see what can be done for her. . . . The next call is to investigate a theft. . . . And you find that one neighbour has accused the other of stealing some garden equipment. . . . After some investigation you find that they have been feuding for years. . . . Next, you investigate a missing female. . . . It's apt to be a sixteen-year-old who has split her home. . . . And the parents cannot understand why she would leave. . . . You find that they have

accused her of being promiscuous and immoral and there have been many quarrels prior to her leaving. . . . You know, all the people figure we got the magic answer and we can make everything normal right away.

Any of the situations listed by the officer could have involved some application of the criminal law. It would take no great legal skill to lay charges against the wife threatening to kill her husband, the neighbour accused of theft, or even the sixteen-year-old who left home. The police, however, are not called for the purpose of laying charges, but rather to defuse trouble.

The criminal law, however, is not written to allow choice. It imposes duties, for violation of which there are penalties. Yet this clearly is at odds with the way police see their job. The law is turned aside to meet the fact that a wife, as an example, is terribly upset. The challenge for the police is how to help in the return to normalcy.

In its own plodding way, the law is beginning to recognize the discretion exercised by the police. The law is beginning to make legitimate what the police have been doing for years. For the police and the community this is good, for it allows standards to be evolved in the use of power. It permits the police and the community to judge action against the law objectively and openly.

Discretion so conferred strips power of the taint of corruption. The police do not have to keep secrets either from themselves or from the citizenry.

This is what a working paper for the Law Reform Commission of Canada had to say:

> When people feel threatened or annoyed by the bizarre or irrational conduct of another, they usually call the police. So the mentally ill's first official contact with the criminal process is often in the person of a police officer. The traditional police response, where the evidence is sufficient, is to dispose of the incident through charging. This should not always be the case; in appropriate circumstances the police should divert the mentally ill away from the criminal process.
>
> Sometimes they do. Police can exercise their discretion (as they do in many other instances) not to charge a mentally ill person who has apparently committed an offence. As well, most provinces empower police to take persons "apparently suffering from mental disorder" into custody without charging and to take them to a hospital.

The law gives the police the power either to lay a criminal charge or to initiate a hospital placement. The differences are enormous. In jail there is penal custody and the likelihood that the illness may fester. In the hospital there can be care, treatment and an easing of tension. The choice is up to the police. The question is how that choice should be exercised. To what extent can the police call upon the community, which has given them the power, for help? Are there simple, speedy procedures for consultation with local hospitals and psychiatric facilities? This much is clear: when the problem arises, it must be handled. A decision must be made. If there is threatening behaviour at 2 A.M. on Saturday, the police cannot wait until 9:00 A.M. on Monday for an answer.

Quebec is attempting an approach. In Montreal a consulting centre was established, the Philippe Pinel Institute of Psychiatry. Police are able to refer persons suspected of mental illness to the centre for preliminary diagnosis. In 1974 the centre received almost 1,000 referrals from the police. Nearly three-quarters were diverted out of the criminal process and back into the community, either directly or after a short period of hospitalization. Nearly 750 persons did not have to suffer the trauma of jail and the stigma of wrongdoing because the police and another social service agency of the community co-operated.

Out of the co-operation comes a feeling of legitimacy. The police are not acting alone in deciding whether to deny a person liberty. An officer does not have to risk the guilt that might come from a hasty and wrong judgment. Moreover, the results of their action can be evaluated in terms of helping a particular person, rather than in adding to the crime statistics.

It is co-operation, not confrontation that the police want. They have no choice. They cannot hide from the community they are intended to serve. If they are to be effective, they must be responsive. The volume of their work requires this. Consider the statistics. There are about 2.2 milion persons living in Metropolitan Toronto. In 1977 the Metropolitan Toronto police had 3.7 million individual contacts. Let this statistic be understood: the police had direct, interpersonal contact on the job with 3.7 million persons.

These contacts were made by a police force that numbers 6,734 persons and operates with a budget of $156.7 million. The numbers and the budget do not appear to be large relative to the work done. And, it should be noted, of the total dollar figure about $124 million is spent on wages and salaries. Little is left for planning. For example, the police were able to allocate only $124,000 to the category of "emergency planning projects" that could include plans to handle disasters, man-made or natural, or acts of terrorism.

The same Metropolitan force, following the recommendations of Arthur Maloney, later the Ontario Ombudsman, established a citizen complaint bureau, headed by a superintendent. The complaint bureau is not a police station, nor is it located in a police station. It is a separate building located in the very centre of the city. More to the point, it is open to receive complaints seven days a week. The officer in charge is required to report monthly to the governing police commission through the chief of police.

The police are daily exposed to the community; the figures on police-community contact in Toronto demonstrate this. Yet of more than 3.7 million citizen-police contacts, only 849, or .02 per cent, resulted in formal complaints against the police.

Working with the Community: Crime Prevention

For the police the challenge is how to meet community expectations, how to be an effective part of the community. Inspector R. M. Heywood of the RCMP spoke on this:

> Let's look at how the police developed over a hundred and fifty years or so in the western world when we had smaller communities. . . . We went through this watch system where somebody from the community was appointed as policeman. Then we got into the full-time policeman. He was drawn from the community, too. He went into it with a lot of local knowledge, a lot of local identification. He was going to investigate things that came to his attention, to solve them. And this became the work ethic, the methodology of police from early times, that he spend his time pursuing offenders, trying to solve crimes and bring the offender to court. He had a good success rate; his solve-rate was higher because he had local knowledge.

No doubt this is true, but the community of a century or a half century ago was smaller than the large cities of today. Then there was a better informal support system of friends and neighbours than social agencies can now provide in the large cities where most Canadians live. Today the task of urban police is far more difficult. But in the view of Inspector Heywood, it is not an impossible goal. He spoke of achieving police integration into the community and the benefits that can follow:

> I would like to tell you about our experiences in North Vancouver. We had some problems with young people. So we decided to go directly to them and see what they thought about it. So we went to the schools. There was a little hesitancy in the beginning. They thought we were going to come in with some kind of hard line. They kind of looked at us and said, "Are you going to develop informers or stool pigeons in here, or what?" And we said no, that were concerned with the problems of this community: that crime is growing, and we've got hostilities towards the police. (The situation was such, in one particular area, that they would gather around a street corner and pitch a rock through a store window and then they'd wait until a police car would drive up. They'd say, "Hey, it took you two minutes longer to get here than it did

yesterday. You'd better smarten up." They'd all laugh. They'd all get a big kick out of this you see. The policemen would get very frustrated because it was one of that group that threw the rock.)

We talked to the teachers and we talked to the counsellors and we talked to student councils. Then we started going into the class-rooms. I went around and did this for about three or four months taking other policemen with me. We said what can we do about this; what's wrong with the policing? They said, "What's the matter with you guys? We don't know you. We don't know anything about you. You're strangers every one of you. Every time a policeman drives along and there's a couple of kids standing on the corner, they roll down the window and say, 'Hey you — come here!' How many kids on the North Shore are called 'Hey you'?" You know, I think that was pretty accurate. Maybe the kids had just said some uncomplimentary things to the policeman as he rolled down the window. I think that happens too; and they admitted this. It was an understanding reached at the time that this wasn't helping either one of us. And in time, after constant involvement here, all this disappeared.

Not all programmes are so successful. High density city neigh-bourhoods require a special effort. Because the usual friend and neigh-bour support is lacking, the social agencies are more important than ever. Inspector Heywood outlined the way in which his department sought to know and be known by people and social agencies:

We meet with community organizations, ratepayer meetings, any kind of kids' groups, teen groups, drop-in centres and so on, and discuss. This is all done by policemen in those zones, who get a little better understanding about what the whole problem is all about and what are some of the solutions. How do you get involvement drawing these agencies together and getting involved with them? Now I don't know whether the police should be sort of a catalyst in the community and try and draw these groups together, but my view is that if it leads to a reduction in crime, then do it. Because that's the name of the game as far as I am concerned.

Not all police accept the necessity of involvement with the com-munity. Many see themselves as law enforcers catching criminals. Relative to the population their force may be few in number, but they can concentrate power and they know the problem areas, and they have a sense of what is expected of them. For example, the Toronto subway system experienced a rash of purse snatchings and assaults, and the gathering of groups of rowdy youths on subway platforms. The press reported the stories and a certain fear began to develop.

The police responded. They stepped up subway surveillance. The police squad responsible consisted of only about seven or eight men, both black and white, working in plain clothes in stations and trains. They showed themselves at trouble spots and broke up loitering youth gangs. The word went out: the police were "everywhere." Disturbances became infrequent and gangs moved their activity to shoplifting and purse snatching above ground. (The assaults tended to decrease somewhat.) Because the activities were above ground, they were more visible and easier to deal with. The police were back to the old game of cops and robbers instead of gang threats underground.

There is little doubt that conflict exists within many police forces as to the appropriate model for police work. Inspector Heywood speaks for police who see themselves as social service representatives, rather than strict law enforcement officers:

> I hear a policeman say, "How can you afford to spend manpower on things like that? You should be solving crime." Well I am. If crime is going down then this is what we are after. In the first three months of last year we had something like 750 crimes left over after we'd solved all we could. This year we had only 600 left over after we'd solved all we could. So I would say the situation is better. Now whether we solved the same percentage or not isn't very important any more, because the unsolved ones are going down.

The results of an attempt by the Metropolitan Toronto Police force for closer ties with the community are equally heartening. The force instituted a programme of "Community Service Officers" (CSO). Very briefly the programme installed police in a particular area and then left them to establish contact with the community. It was much more than a "beat" or a "patrol": the officers were highly involved in the community and established formal and informal contacts. The aim was to forge a new relation between community and police so that problems could be solved, together. The officers worked with neighbourhood groups, social agencies, hostels and drop-in centres.

In a real sense, the ultimate goal was to motivate communities to take care of themselves so that the CSO would not be needed. The programme has a reasonable measure of success. Perhaps nowhere is this sort of contact more crucial than between ethnic groups and the police, particularly in the context of Canada's large immigrant population. One youth who was exposed to the CSO had come to Canada from the United States. He called himself a "revolutionary." His was a rather curious complaint: "If we are going to avoid what is happening south of border, they better get a whole lot more people like the CSO here in Toronto . . . because that is the only thing that is going to stop it at all. They are the only tool we have to increase the understanding between the two cultures at the moment and . . . well . . . they are all we've got."

The CSO programme demonstrates sharply the nexus between crime prevention and an understanding of the community. To illustrate, consider the lengths the police were prepared to go to prevent "crime" at Nathan Phillips Square.

It was summer. There was a rock concert being held in the square. The permit for the gathering expired at 5:00 P.M. The main attraction had not arrived; it was held up at Canadian Customs. Phone calls were made to two City Hall officials; both refused to extend the permit. The police, in their own way, refused to let the decision stand. They knew what the results of a premature cancellation of the concert would be. The police, in effect, threatened City Hall. They said they would withdraw and would not be responsible for any damage or injury. It would be the fault of City Hall for failing to heed the experts. The police won the argument and the permit was extended, defusing a potentially explosive situation. The police prevented crime; they understood the community; they used their power with discretion.

At any number of levels, it is possible to criticize the police. Locally, incidents of brutality and bias have surfaced and have been proved. Nationally, the RCMP have been implicated in unlawful bugging, arson, and theft — all in the name of national security. For all this, the fact remains that by a considerable margin Canadians believe the police, locally and nationally, are doing a good job. In a 1978 poll of thirty-two Canadian cities, 64 per cent rated their local police as either good or excellent, while 27 per cent rate them as adequate. The popularity of the RCMP is somewhat lower. Sixty-one per cent gave them a good to excellent rating, and 19 per cent found them adequate. A vast majority (80 per cent) think local police are honest and courteous. Only 27 per cent believed that police are "capable" of bias or prejudice.

It is doubtful that any other segment of the criminal justice system, from Crown attorneys, to courts, to correctional institutions, could pull such a high rating. What is even more telling is the fact that the police alone have such direct, ongoing contact with the community. And this offers a unique opportunity for the police to share in an open way their concerns with the community, to let the community know the limitations and the capacities of the force. We can hope that eventually the community will begin to take a larger share of responsibility. Professor Herman Goldstein wrote:

> Factors like the birth rate, unemployment, the sense of community that exists in a given neighbourhood and even the weather probably have more to do with the incidence of crime than do the police.
> Yet most view the inability of the police to deal with these problems as a failure. To avoid such criticism, the police often attempt the impossible. Aside from inviting more criticism, such responses perpetuate public expectations that are unrealistic.

The police must ask themselves if presenting a tough, albeit undefined, stance is of such importance that it offsets the cost in not sharing with the community a more precise description of police capabilities. Greater openness regarding their true capacity in handling various aspects of their business would greatly reduce the pressures now brought to bear upon the police. It would increase the willingness of the public to provide the additional resources when such a need is demonstrated. And it would increase the likelihood that the public would more aggressively explore alternatives for dealing with some of the problems now relegated to the police — a development which is long overdue.

In themselves, the police are a potent force. By the end of 1976 they totalled 51,629 men and women. Expressed somewhat differently, they numbered one police officer for every four hundred Canadians. First-class constables with five or more years' experience earned about $20,000 annually. The overall bill to Canadians for police salaries in 1976 was about $1 billion. Supporting the police is a civilian group of 12,046 people.

The police are part of the community. They have views concerning crime and police enforcement. They have associations that speak for them in their role as police officers. And the associations can and do argue for policies, and changes in law. Recently several police groups have lobbied the public and Parliament for a return to capital punishment. Let murderers hang; it is not enough to sentence those guilty to a maximum term of twenty-five years in prison.

A study for the Law Reform Commission of Canada stated: "If [police] officers have the opportunity to discuss their job and their perception of public morals and values, it becomes evident that they generally have a comprehensive appraisal of their communities' attitudes." The police generally do mirror public feelings. Should their associations be allowed to promote their views as to what ought to be public policy?

The police stand as a military force. In a democratic society such a force is and must be subject to civilian rule. The elected representatives are responsible to the people, and the police, as civil servants, are responsible to the elected representatives and, more important, to the faithful implementation of law. For the police as an *organized* group to question the law or its enforcement, outside of the line of governmental accountability, raises a serious question. It is a challenge to command, and, as such, a challenge to civilian control. It is as if the police were to say: "We know best because we are the police."

On the issue of capital punishment the police are wrong not only in their *organized* lobbying, but also in the substantive argument they make. The facts are that most murderers are *not* mindless, mad dog killers, who can be stopped only by the threat of the death penalty. The facts are that most murders in Canada arise out of family disputes. Editorially the *Sunday Star* spoke to the point when it related the stories of three "typical" murderers serving life sentences in Canadian prisons in 1978. All were sentenced to be hanged, and all of them spent time on death row before their sentences were commuted. (Their names and some of the minor details are changed to mask their identities.)

• John, a highly intelligent man in his fifties, is an engineer. He shot his girlfriend's husband. On the day of the shooting John learned that the husband had learned of the affair and was after him with a gun. John took a gun, left his house, and saw the husband across the street. The husband yelled at John, who thought he was in danger. John drew his gun and killed the husband, who, as it turned out, was not armed. John was charged with murder and convicted.

• Bill's marriage was difficult in no small measure because of his tangled monetary affairs. Once he and his wife quarreled. Their anger was sharp and heated. Neighbours called the police. By the time the police arrived, Bill had had too many beers. When the constable asked him to quiet down, Bill took his hunting rifle and fired. The constable was killed. Bill was sentenced to death and spent six months on death row before his sentence was commuted to life imprisonment.

Eight years after the murder, Bill has become a skilled photographer. He is often allowed to visit Toronto where he frequents photographers' studios. He has difficulty seeing himself as a "cop killer."

• Ned killed his girlfriend in a jealous rage. He was nineteen. Ten years later Ned has earned a Bachelor of Arts degree. He did this the hard way, first through correspondence courses, and then through limited prison furloughs. He is very different from the uncontrolled, impulsive creature who killed his girlfriend so many years before.

The *Sunday Star* concluded:

When asked why the knowledge they would be hanged had not deterred them, all three men say they were completely out of control at the time. Fear, panic, jealousy and drugs made them indifferent to consequences of their act.

All three would have hung if the government had not been determined to avoid enforcing the death penalty.

Now that you know something about John, Bill and Ned are you willing to see them hang? Would you feel any safer if they were to be executed?

Will it really benefit this country if politicians portray these men as monsters in order to win some extra votes?

Many police associations would have government order the death of these three "typical" murderers. Yet the facts speak against their execution. How could rational, professional police officers believe that hanging, as such, would deter crime?

Police officers are not necessarily experts in crime prevention. Nor do they necessarily understand the basic value system that underlies the Canadian system of government. They are people given a difficult, often unrewarding job. They are given this job with limited formal training. They learn how to handle weapons, understand basic law, follow commands, and investigation procedures. They learn all these things in a short, intense training period.

The real education of the police is on the street. The public should understand this. To do their job well the police need not only citizen co-operation, but also acceptance of the fact that both citizen and police must learn together. Both must learn to be open to facts, to know that solutions to crime may not be so easy as resorting to the hangman's knot. They must learn that solutions must be developed inside a democratic imperative. There are values in a free society that should be preserved.

There is little the police cannot do if the community, the courts, and the state are working together to ensure enforcement of the law. This does not mean that at certain points there will not be frustration. An entire community can be terrorized by the acts of a few. What co-operation means, however, is participation in the achievement of common goals in which all play a role and, in so doing, enjoy the respect of their fellow citizens.

CHAPTER
FIVE

Hard Times: The Prison System

"Many in the community have the misconception that, once the offenders are sentenced, that is the end of it; . . . they never come out and therefore cannot cause trouble again. The reality is that all — except those who die in prison — come out legally on expiration of their sentence. . . . Therefore it is apparent that the community is safer if the person who shares their freedom is not more dangerous when he rejoins them in life on the outside." Canadian Parliamentary Subcommittee on Prisons.

Prisoner Profile

There is a myth that the criminal justice system is lax: too many of the guilty go free. It may be that many of those who should be in prison are not, but the reason has little to do with the sentencing disposition of Canadian judges. If the guilty go free, it may have to do with the failure of victims to report crimes, the inability of police to find the evidence, including willing witnesses, and the need for the Crown prosecutor to plea bargain.

The statistics relating to imprisonment in Canada are dramatic. They give the lie to the myth of laxity. In Canada today, on any given day, about one in every thousand residents is serving time in a penal institution. There are at any given time 20,000 imprisoned adult offenders. About 75,000 persons are imprisoned each year in federal, provincial, or municipal jails.

What are the crimes which bring Canada to the level of having more persons in prison than most other western nations? "Close to one-half of the 4,000 persons sent to penitentiaries each year are serving sentences for having committed non-violent offences against property or the public order. Indeed, less than 20 per cent of offenders are imprisoned for having committed acts of violence against the person. Statistics reveal similar results in respect of provincial institutions. . . . Almost 50 per cent of prisoners in some provincial institutions were imprisoned because they could not pay fines."

Perhaps, however, the convicted are hardened felons. Perhaps they are sent to prison because there is no other way to deal with them. The reality does not reflect this. One out of every seven persons appearing in court for the first time in Canada and convicted of a non-violent offence against property is imprisoned. On a second conviction for a non-violent property offence almost 50 per cent of offenders are imprisoned.

There is another way to ask the question of who is imprisoned. Put simply, are the wealthy treated differently than the poor? The answer is clearly yes. Consider by way of example the story of a twenty-five-year-old woman who, with her husband, brought more than $500,000 worth of hard drugs into Canada. She was apprehended and charged. Her family had wealth and could afford high-priced legal counsel and psychiatric consultation. It could also afford $50,000 in bail. More than a year passed between arrest and trial. In that time the accused found a job, with the help of her family, and obtained psychiatric help. When the trial came, her counsel was able to plea bargain a greatly reduced charge. When she was sentenced, counsel was able to demonstrate a desire on the part of the accused to rehabilitate herself, and to offer effective psychiatric testimony to counter the pre-sentence report of the Crown. In the result, the accused was given a suspended sentence. Her crime was serious, but her family's money bought her a different kind of justice than is afforded the poor.

A national report stated:

> In theory crimes are crimes and punished equally no matter who commits them. In practice the penalty depends, not on the nature of the crime, but on the person who commits it. Our prison population, for example, contains a quite unrepresentative proportion of poor, of disadvantaged and of native offenders. The richer you are, the better your chance of getting away with something. Is it that the rich make the laws and so what rich men do is not a crime but simply shrewd business practice? Or is it that position and wealth protect the rich against intervention? Certainly more poor than rich are prosecuted even on a proportional reckoning. Or is it that those who can afford expensive lawyers have better hope of being acquitted? For all the respect we pay to justice and equality, we still have one law for the rich and another for the poor.

Most prisoners, then, are not violent at the time of arrest, trial or conviction. They have committed crimes against property. They come from the ranks of the poor and the disadvantaged. What does prison do to them?

The specific descriptions are chilling. Newspapers have described thirty-inch cells, windowless corridors, brutal guards, internal violence. These are not the views of a few. Nor are they a reflection of the distant past.

Inside the Prison: Violence

From time to time Canadian prison conditions, particularly in maximum security institutions, become so intolerable that the situation explodes violently. A federal parliamentary subcommittee described the crises that led to its creation:

Seven years of comparative peace in the Canadian Penitentiary System ended in 1970 with a series of upheavals (riots, strikes, murders and hostage takings) that grew in number and size with each passing year. By 1976 the prison explosions were almost constant; hardly another week passed without another violent incident. The majority were in Canada's maximum security institutions. In the 42 years between 1932 and 1974 there were a total of 65 major incidents in federal penitentiaries. Yet in two years — 1975-1976 — there was a total of 69 major incidents including 35 hostage-taking incidents involving 92 victims, one of whom (a prison officer) was killed.

. . . The eruption and violence were born of anger, frustration and oppression within the tight and unnatural confines of prison over unresolved grievances, transfers, harassment and provocation described by both sides [staff and inmates in adversary attitudes] as "mind games."

It is impossible to measure the full cost to the Canadian people, not only of the damage and excessive overtime, but also in injury and death.

It is also impossible, it should be noted, to calculate the damage done to the system of justice in this country. Nor is it possible to measure the effect on the public conscience and consciousness. The parliamentary subcommittee consisted of members of all parties. Most of its report and recommendations were unanimous. Yet the government has left large portions of its recommendations untouched, and there has been no significant public outcry. It may be that the public is unconcerned. It may be that the public sees no threat to itself. In its report, handed down in 1977, the parliamentary subcommittee issued a cold warning to the public:

Many in the community have the misconception that, once the offenders are sentenced, that is the end of it; they are out of sight and out of life; they never come out and therefore cannot cause trouble again.

The reality is that all — except those who die in prison — come out legally on expiration of their sentence. The federal system receives all those with sentences of two years and over; the provincial system, those two years less a day and under. The longest sentence is usually life, or twenty-five years, before parole is possible.

When they come out they are the people who move into the house or apartment next door, who ride buses with you, eat in the next booth in restaurants, walk on the same streets, sell papers, deliver groceries, fill your gas tanks, and talk about the weather with you in the theatre line-up.

Therefore it is apparent that the community is safer if the person who shares their freedom is not more dangerous when he rejoins them in life on the outside. Prisons, as they now exist, protect society only during the two, three, ten or twenty years the inmate is in there; but if the institutions are boring, oppressive and lack programs preparing the inmates for release, they come out angry, vindictive, frustrated, snarling like animals released from long confinement in a cage. Many are released onto the streets directly from maximum security institutions, unadjusted, unprepared, with fear, tension and paranoia that spell danger to the community.

There is little in the system to stimulate inmates to reform, to correct the behavior and morality that brought them into prison. Thus the Canadian Penitentiary Service has failed the Canadians who paid highly and must continue to pay for reformative processes that they can only hope can succeed inside the big wall.

Most of those in prison are not dangerous. However, cruel lockups, isolation, the injustices and harassment deliberately inflicted on prisoners unable to fight back, make non-violent inmates violent, and those already dangerous more dangerous.

It is a fact that life in prison is hard time both for prisoners and guards. Let the members of Parliament, a group not specially identified with prisoner rights, speak of the evidence which they gathered:

The Sub-Committee even heard evidence concerning guards who have given known slashers razor blades and taunted them to slash themselves. On occasion the inmates have done as they were told. At the B.C. Penitentiary at least nine inmates in one range slashed themselves on Christmas Eve 1976 after a guard left two razor blades in a cell and told them to "have a Merry Christmas and a slashing New Year."

To the inmates, the correctional officers are the visible instruments of the system that keeps them locked into a life, as well as a place, of directionless and frustrating idleness. These officers are regarded by some prisoners as "fair game" for continuing insults, abuse, minor physical annoyances and all the other manifestations of anger in a system with no constructive outlet and few other targets. In the absence of the stability and self-assurance that come from good training and a sense of professionalism, this behaviour has become reciprocal, with the staff and inmates locked into what amounts to an endless and mutually-destructive low-level verbal and psychological warfare. This often sparks into violence, as happened at the Millhaven, Laval and British Columbia Penitentiaries. It continues over the months and years, as each side seeks the empty triumph of goading the other into reprisals. This imposes an almost unendurable strain on everyone in a penitentiary, whether employed or imprisoned there. More than any other single factor, it diverts the energies of all concerned away from any goals essential to the self-esteem of both sides.

Pressure and tension are constant on staff; the fear of making a mistake which could result in an escape, a hostage-taking situation, or some other form of violence, is always present. Threats are regularly received by staff — sometimes from friends of inmates or former inmates, sometimes from fellow staff members. Many of them keep weapons at home and have unlisted telephone numbers. Reported incidents are rare but those that have occurred were serious.

Staff perceive themselves as having fewer rights than inmates. They resent the erosion of their power over the inmates. Increased access by outside groups to the institutions, open visits, Inmate Committees, new programs, the presence of contraband and generally the lack of discipline and increased freedom of inmates are seen by correctional officers as causing a deterioration in security.

The self-image of correctional officers is poor. They do not see themselves as important contributors to penal justice but only as watchmen who contain men and ensure that they do not escape or do harm. The job provides little intellectual challenge or sense of achievement. They blame their poor community image on the media. They resent the perceived lack of management support. They admit they are ashamed of their jobs. The result is bitterness, low morale, disloyalty, loss of confidence and loss of pride both in their work and in the Service, which in turn accelerate the burning out of staff.

The ultimate weapon of the custodial officers is "security," and it can be — and has been — used quite effectively by the staff to demonstrate, not only to the inmates but also to themselves, that they are the final masters, in physical terms. We find when matters have gone beyond the unprofessionally narrow limits of tolerance of the custodial staff, that their response tends to be an insistence on tighter and more rigid security. When this happens, not only do the work and socialization programs begin to suffer, but also the prison atmosphere becomes more than usually oppressive and potentially explosive. The suggestion

given by Dragan Cernetic, former Director of the British Columbia
Penitentiary, put an important point succinctly: "security comes first,
but inmate programs are more important." It is essential that this
perspective prevail in the penitentiary system, although at present it
unfortunately does not.

Custodial officers' inclination towards solving inmate-staff problems
through increased security measures is often based on a not-unfounded
apprehension for their own safety. They become trapped in a
purposeless confrontation with men, many of whom have
demonstrated an inability to control their potential for violence, and
some of whom, like those imprisoned under the new twenty-five-year
no-parole sentences, may feel they have nothing to lose. In addition,
however, to their own safety and reasonable considerations of control
of movement and function, we find that much of the insistence on
increased security stems from other factors; they all have a cumulative
corrosive effect on the penitentiary system.

Security assumes many forms. Sometimes "security considerations"
become the reason why clean laundry is not available to inmates for
weeks at a time. The sudden necessity to count and re-count, while the
inmates wait in frustration and suppressed rage over what appears to
be — and often is — intentional harassment, is another expression of
tighter security. Inmates are sometimes awakened every hour by a
custodial officer's keys or a boot banging on their cell doors on the
pretext of a check that the inmates are present there and alive. There is
an extraordinary disproportion between any realistic evaluation of the
probability of escape and the zeal with which it is guarded against, and
the practice is unknown in U.S. federal institutions. Inmates are also
sometimes awakened at night by a staff member playing with the lights.
We also heard evidence of staff at several institutions delaying meals
and occasionally contaminating the food before it was delivered to
inmates. [Inmates have sometimes also contaminated the food of staff
members in the most gross ways when they have had the opportunity.]

The raison d'etre of the penitentiary system ought to be primarily
the successful re-integration into society of the inmates. This, however,
is easily lost sight of by those whose energies must be mainly devoted to
self protection and survival in what can sometimes only be accurately
described as a nerve-racking jungle. "In this 'them or us' situation, the
choice . . . is generally dictated by immediate self-interest rather than by
any long-term or theoretical concern for the inmates' eventual return
to the community or the problems that Canadian society, however
imperfectly, is attempting to deal with through its penitentiary
system."

Reform: Questionable

Is there any way to improve the staff's position? Would the addition of more staff do the job? In 1977 the Canadian Penitentiary Service had 9,020 staff members looking after 9,401 prisoners. This is almost a one to one ratio.

Research several years ago monitored a group of newly hired shop instructors who came to prison to teach inmates in a vocational rehabilitation programme and who, at the outset, were eager, full of ideas and very optimistic about their jobs. Two years later, tests and interviews showed the group to be sadly depleted, out of ideas and effectively "institutionalized." In addition, it was found that their functional vocabulary level had dropped by an average of 50 per cent. It's hard to resist the steady onslaught of chronic inmate discontent, public censure and statistics forever proving that every new idea or plan is failing.

Andreas Schroeder is a Canadian poet who has done time in several of this nation's prisons, and written a book, *Shaking It Rough,* about his experiences. (The title, in prison jargon, means doing hard time.) He gives an inside, highly personal view of the prison system and the people who run it.

Being in prison slowly began to feel more and more as if I'd been dropped down the hopper of some huge, numbing, unpredictable, implacable and unopposable machine, an apparatus so depersonalized and so unwieldy that even those in control of it didn't ever really expect it to work.
[For the Corrections system isn't only extraordinarily inefficient, it's also filled to a large extent with personnel who have for all intents and purposes given up, who frankly don't give much of a damn anymore] . . .
[It is the combination of this administration lethargy and inmate distress, of staff members who can no longer care and inmates who are desperate to get out but can only make their applications and appeals through that same staff, which finally leads to the sense of futility and dejection that permeates every prison in which I've done my time, and without doubt, every prison in North America. It's the source of most of the cynicism and hypocrisy that pervade modern day jails, and it's ultimately another major reason for the Corrections system's failure to solve its part of the Crime Cycle problem.]

The public views discussion of prison reform with some suspicion. It suspects a "soft" attitude toward law breakers. It feels that law breakers deserve punishment. But consider and weigh the punishment given. Read the story of Jenny White, reported by Olivia Ward in the *Toronto Star.* Ms. White spoke of two kinds of women in Kingston prison — the ones waiting for parole and those who have given up hope as if they were waiting for death. "You get down in prison. . . . The longer you're inside the worse it gets. Sometimes you're so down you think you'll never crawl outside again and see the light. You just shrivel up and die inside."

When she was nineteen, jailed at Kingston Prison for Women for a first offence, heroin possession, Jenny saw prison turn women into "zombies." In her two and a half years as an inmate in Canada's only federal women's prison, she learned, "Jail doesn't work. People get apathetic, not rehabilitated, in that place. If you're strong enough you can pull yourself out of it. But when you're alone, isolated, surrounded by people you know are out to get you, it takes an awful lot of strength. You break down."

Arrested in Edmonton in 1973, Jenny was shipped to Kingston, more than 2,500 miles away, because her five-year sentence was over the two-year limit for provincial jails. "That's the big problem," she said. "Maybe 70 per cent of people at Kingston are on drug charges. They're a pretty meek-and-mild bunch. They don't want to hassle. But the others are rough and tough — they're repeaters, lifers, women who've committed manslaughter, violent crimes, robbery. We called them the Heavies."

The heavies are well-known to prison staff at Kingston. Most have been in jail more than five years. When the staff members ignore the bloody noses, cuts and bruises and the screams of inmates who "accidentally" fall down the stairs after a difference of opinion with the heavies, Jenny said, "That's when I began to know what real loneliness was. Nobody hears. Nobody cares. Outside, nobody knows." But there are more subtle dangers from exposing first offenders to hardened criminals, she said. "A lot of young girls get weak. They suck up to the Heavies for protection. They learn all kinds of rackets from them — you hear them talking about forgery a lot, and how they can hardly wait to get out and try some new method they'd never heard about before."

Therapy and counselling are almost unknown at Kingston, she said. "The prison psychiatrist hands out tranquillizers. Some women save them up so they can get high later." The prison court, chaired by the director, gives inmates who run afoul of rules informal "sentences."

"You can lose your day or weekend pass, or get some kind of minor penalty. But no amount of discipline can get to the roots of the problem." That, says Jenny, is getting the violent heavies away from the others, and helping non-violent inmates and first offenders to get back into the community as soon as possible. "Prison breeds violence," said Jenny. "Whether you want to kill yourself or somebody else, it's all part of the same destructive system."

What is the purpose of placing people in prison? In direct costs, approximately $14,000 to $17,000 dollars a year (depending on the institution) are spent to imprison a single law-breaker. In addition, society accepts the indirect expense of maintaining a prisoner's family on welfare. What is the purpose of this spending?

Is the aim to provide a moral lesson? To show criminals that they did something wrong? It doesn't happen. In prisons the comment can be heard on every side: "You know the difference between me and the guy on the outside? I got caught!"

The person is punished, not for breaking the law, but for the fact of being caught. Prison is not the result of a moral certainty — it is the wheel of fortune.

Will imprisonment instil respect for the criminal justice system? "There is a great deal of irony [and tragedy] in the fact that imprisonment — the ultimate product of our system of criminal justice — itself epitomizes injustice."

When penitentiaries were first established by the Philadelphia Quakers in 1789, they were seen as a more humane alternative to the harsh punishments of the day. The Quakers believed that isolation with opportunities for work and religious contemplation would render the offender penitent and reformed. How far have we come since the first Canadian prison was established in Kingston in 1835?

Our prisons today certainly are not places for work and contemplation. They are Alice in Wonderland holding cells for the training of more hardened criminals. There are long enforced periods of boredom; there is little opportunity to learn a trade; there is less opportunity to earn money. The most that a federal prisoner may earn is about $13.50 a month.

Most prisoners serve time; they do not participate in work-release programmes. And for those serving time the pressures are enormous.

The prisoner is not expected to pay taxes as free citizens do, or to pay restitution or fulfill other obligations expected of citizens. In undermining the offender's self-image and depriving him of the opportunities to help sustain his family, pay his debts and contribute to unemployment and pension funds, prisons add to the burdens of society as a whole. . . . News reports of suicides and attempted suicides and of violence in prisons give further reality to another aspect of the pressures of prison life.

Loss of respect arises as well from the closed nature of the prison or correction system. It lacks sufficient visibility and public accountability. Decision-making in corrections until recently was generally beyond outside review and complaints about unfairness were handled by the correctional branch in its own setting.

At the same time it is known that while the officials are in charge of penal institutions, it is at least partially true that large security prisons can only be run with the co-operation and tacit consent of the prisoners. There are understood limits beyond which the administration may go only at its peril. Yet the almost invisible and non-accountable nature of the prisoners' power results in tension, coercion and injustice within the institutions.

One of the tools of coercion is the prison system's ability to vary the length of a prisoner's stay. This covers not only parole, but also the privilege of a few days outside the prison on a "temporary absence," and even the ambiguity that may be written into the judge's sentence. This uncertainty is one of the factors contributing to the unrest in penitentiaries.

It is a thorny problem for all the actors in this drama: guards can use the power to grant or withhold freedom for leverage and power; prisoners can lose sight of what outsiders might think their "logical" aim, to get back into the community; the community can fear convicts re-entering the community.

Work and Release

Consider the much criticized "Temporary Absences" programme. Introduced in 1961, it allows prison directors to grant passes of up to three days to inmates who are considered good risks for rehabilitative or humanitarian purposes. The programme enjoyed success. The rate of safe return was over 99 per cent. By 1972 the annual number of passes granted had reached 65,000. The next year the figure was cut in half as a result of public outrage over the murder of a prison guard's six-year-old daughter by a convicted murderer out on a pass. That murder represented an infinitesimally small percentage of failure but community fear was great. The programme was curtailed.

If the purpose of prison is to detain certain dangerous people, away from society where they can do harm, then surely they should serve a full term. Yet in 1972, 84.1 per cent of those paroled had not served half of their sentence before being returned to society. Does this mean the state is generous? Remember that less than 20 per cent of prisoners are guilty of crimes against the person. As such, they don't seem to pose a great risk to society, while the benefits of parole to the corrections system are great.

Simply in economic terms, parole is far cheaper than imprisonment. Estimates range from as high as 32 to 35 *times* cheaper (Fateux Report 1956) to a low of 7.2 to 16.3 times cheaper (National Parole Board, *Annual Report* 1967-1968). It lessens the overcrowding in the prisons, which eases the difficulties of the guards.

Further, parole can be used as a club to ensure prison docility. Inmates in an Ontario penitentiary were asked: "How are inmates here affected by knowing there is a chance of parole?" One inmate said: "It is always in your mind like a fantasy — you're always aware of it. Your spirits are higher until you are turned down, when you become very depressed, feeling you weren't done right by. You become antagonistic." Another replied: "Many really worry. It is held over their heads like blackmail."

Public awareness of parole is not, however, determined by its successes. (The Ontario Board of Parole in reporting on the year ending March 31, 1974, declared that 72 per cent of paroles were completed successfully.) It is often measured by its worst failures. James Tolan is such a failure.

> There is not much about Edward James Tolan to inspire trust. There is, on the other hand, much that would inspire fear and suspicion because this is a manifestly dangerous man whose criminal record goes back to 1949. . . . Why then was Tolan given bail last August 11, pending trial on charges of conspiring to commit robbery, assaulting police and possessing a dangerous weapon?
>
> The question assumes very great importance because Tolan killed while on bail. He has just been sentenced to fifteen years in penitentiary for the manslaughter of Ann Hardy, a thirty-four-year-old drug addict with whom he was living.
>
> Tolan had killed before. In 1966 he was sentenced to six years in penitentiary for the shotgun manslaughter of a twenty-nine-year-old Brantford man. By 1970 he was out on parole and he was on probation when arrested on the robbery conspiracy. Chronologically, the sequence goes like this: offence, jail, parole, offence, bail, offence, jail.

Public pressure can manifest itself in the courtroom. The parole system can affect the sentence handed down by the judge. In a study done of Ontario magistrates, forty-two of seventy-one respondents (59.2 per cent) admitted that "they sometimes increased the length of the sentence imposed . . . in light of the possibility of parole being granted."

This division of sentencing power between court and parole board, is explored by Professor Norval Morris:

> More importantly, one latent function of parole must be mentioned. The judge imposes sentence at a time of high emotional response to the facts of crime. Even within our grossly dilatory system of justice, the sentence follows closely upon the public narration of the criminal events, if not upon the commission of the crime. A parole board, however may make its decision in what one hopes will be a less punitive social atmosphere. One important latent purpose of probation is to allow a judge to give the appearance of doing something while in fact doing nothing. Similarly, one latent purpose of the division of

power between judge and parole board is to give the possibility of some clemency while appearing in the public eye to be imposing a more severe punishment.

It is alarming to think parole is being used to deceive the community in some way. The community must understand the process if it is going to succeed. How successful can "reintegration" be if it is done on the sly? As the former Solicitor General, Warren Allmand, states:

The public should be encouraged to learn a bit more about the criminal justice system, to understand what it is and what it is not, what it can and what it cannot do; what can be expected of it and what cannot be expected of it. . . . The public should be encouraged to accept a greater degree of responsibility for the social deviance of individuals and be disabused of the notions that all its behavioural problems can be solved by calling in the police. . . . The public should be disabused of the notion that once the offender is apprehended, tried and convicted and imprisoned, the problem he presents has been solved. . . . The aim of corrections must be to fit them to live successfully within the acceptable limitations of society. . . . At least we have learned that offenders cannot be rehabilitated in prison. In Canada at least, we do not yet seem to have convinced the public that the process of graduated release is not intended as a softening of the sentence for the offender, but is directed at enabling the offender in a controlled series of steps to reintegrate into society, thereby contributing to the protection of society. . . . I wonder if the . . . critics . . . ever contemplate the effects of the alternative — keeping an offender behind bars for two, five, ten or fifteen years and then one morning suddenly releasing him upon society without any supervision, without any hope of doing anything, other than looking up his old criminal friends or the new criminal friends he has made in prison.

Undeniably — unless the community is prepared to kill offenders — there must be acceptance of the fact that they *will* return to society. And when this happens,can there be any doubt that society wants them to be like the majority, namely, law-abiding? This cannot be done by wishful thinking; it can only be done by reintegration. Yet, the community does not seem to operate in its own self-interest. More often than not, there is resistance to the establishment of half-way houses — especially by the neighbourhoods where they would be located. Government finds itself in the position of forcing programmes upon the public. *Time* reported:

Ottawa is also trying to ease prisoners' re-entry into society by setting up hostel-like Community Correctional Centres (CCC) where inmates can serve the last three to six months of their sentences.

Typically, at a CCC over a post office branch on Toronto's Yonge street, some fourteen residents are supervised by ex-penitentiary officer Jim West. They look for jobs or work during the day and receive evening and weekend passes as long as they behave themselves. So far, there are thirteen CCC's in major cities across the country. "I did eleven years in maxs and this is the first time I've felt we are getting down to something worthwhile," says West.

But CCC's have been opposed in Montreal and Moncton, N.B., where community pressure backed by the then-Mayor and city council forced Ottawa to abandon plans for a CCC.

The community would premise the notion of reintegration on "rehabilitation" in prison. But this simply is not workable. To survive in the prison system often demands the kind of compromise and behaviour which makes integration into the community mainstream nearly impossible. In the end, the convicted, the prisoners, find their own rationalization. They condemn the system that sentenced them. They reinforce their own hostility. Andreas Schroeder speaks strongly:

[The court appearance] was my first exposure to a peculiar brand of hypocrisy which I later encountered again and again in the prison system, and which to my mind is a major contributor to much of the failure of the Corrections Department throughout the country.

I'm speaking of this odd insistence on penitence, on remorse and contrition, which seems to be the stock-in-trade of parole boards, courts, religious Corrections groups and prison administrations everywhere; this odd insistence that an inmate must at all costs pretend not to be seen as unrehabilitated; if he makes this plea, his parole (or his pass) is virtually assured. If he doesn't, there are very few boards that are not so rigidly committed to this mother/father-and-child routine ("Come on now; say you're sorry!") that they will not automatically defer his application.

The insincerity and (self) deception this engenders, even encourages, is both mathematically predictable and enormously far-reaching in its effect, and here lies the disaster of the prison system in a nutshell: our prisons are not "schools of crime" in the sense that mixing with "hardened criminals" teaches a new inmate new ways to blow a safe or forge a check (you don't have to go to prison to learn about that; there are books on the subject); they are schools of crime because they teach, they even force, an inmate to become a professional hypocrite in order to survive the place and get out. Because I hadn't then and I haven't since ever met an inmate who was sorry about anything except the fact that he got caught[.But the constant fawning and lying required to negotiate the administrative, bureaucratic and psychiatric hurdles inside are far more ruinous to his psyche than two years of beatings and hard labour might have been. Such hypocrisy is like the worst kind of disease; it spills over and infects an inmate's entire life, and when he finally gets out and tries to manoeuvre himself back onto the rails in Outside society, the automatic distorting and posturing has become a conditioned response which he finds virtually impossible to overcome, assuming he still wants to. Mostly, the attendant troubles of such situations aren't overly long in putting in their appearances and in due course the vicious circle closes with a loud click.

CHAPTER
SIX

A Community Experiment

"It is this Court's intention to substitute the Village of Bancroft for the physical confines of a prison; the members of society [for] your custodial officers; and the terms of a probation order [for] the formalized rules of the institution." **Judge J. L. Clendenning, Ontario Provincial Court, Village of Bancroft.**

Breaking the Crime Cycle

In the end, the community pays a price for its own failure to act. Finally the community must treat with those who violate its laws. There is no escape. Not even the gallows is an escape, for the punishment is one that taints all; it will not be washed away.

The reality of crime, however, has little to do with violence. It has much more to do with acts against property for which imprisonment follows. The typical case, if such it may be called, is that of the young person caught in petty theft, and, after several arrests, sent to a training school. Detention there is not overly long. Following release, the crimes continue. The value of the property stolen may increase. The offender becomes well known to police. There are more arrests, convictions, and prison sentences which usually are shortened by early release for good behaviour.

The circle of crime, arrest, conviction, sentence, release and new crimes continues even until the death of the offender — who seldom becomes wealthy as a result of crimes.

The cost to the community in the life of a single person of the kind described can range from $300,000 to $400,000. This is not an exaggerated figure; it does not even include the indirect costs. It covers only the expense of custodial care over a period of about thirty years at a cost of $14,000 to $17,000 per year, depending on whether the holding institution is federal or provincial.

DISCOUNT JUSTICE

At the end of such a life, what has the community received for all the money it has spent? All that can be said is that for the period when the criminal was in jail, the public was protected. (It is curious to note that the amount spent keeping the accused in jail, more likely than not, far exceeded the amount taken illegally.)

How can the circle be broken? On occasion the frustration level of the courts becomes sufficiently high that turnstile justice gives way to innovation. What follows is the case of a "typical" criminal grown old and before the court for yet another offence.

What makes the case different is the judge. He took the time to innovate. He did not allow the press of his case load to result in still another prison sentence. What the judge did with the accused he has done with others, and, it must be noted, his efforts are appreciated by the police.

Read how the court weighs the problem, and, in the result, compels community participation. The decision was handed down by Judge J. L. Clendenning in the Ontario Provincial Court (Criminal Division), Village of Bancroft, County of Hastings, in 1974. The accused is referred to as Mr. N.

Mr. N. was fifty years old at the time of sentence. His crime was the theft of a truck and contents of a value exceeding two hundred dollars. This is an offence which carries a maximum penalty of up to ten years in prison. The reality of the crime, however, was somewhat less serious. According to the police, Mr. N. simply took a truck full of valuable lumber for a "joy ride." His problems began when the truck was wrecked in an accident. The police felt that they had no choice but to lay charges against Mr. N.

Mr. N. is a thin, small man. He has never given the police "trouble," and they even regard him as a likeable individual. He has never been involved in a crime of violence. What follows, in a somewhat condensed form, is a transcript of the sentence passed on Mr. N. by Judge Clendenning.

HIS HONOUR: The criminal record of the accused was in effect the primary submission by the Crown and is worthy of analysis. It discloses since May 14, 1943, in an approximate thirty-one-year period, the convictions of the accused for forty-three separate criminal offences, for which he was sentenced to a total of almost thirty years in custodial institutions of various types. To reduce it to average, the accused during the past thirty-one years has committed forty-three offences, or almost one-and-one-half per year, and was sentenced to an average of almost one year per year during that period. In addition, the accused was sentenced to a training school at the age of twelve, where he resided until he was fifteen. As the pre-sentence report indicates, the accused has spent more than two-fifths of his lifetime within the confines of some type of custodial institution.

I think on the basis of this information it is fair to say the accused has become what sociologists and psychologists refer to as "institutionalized." By that is meant: without the physical restrictions of a custodial institution and the application of formalized rules regulating virtually every aspect of his existence, the accused is, or has become, incapable of operating effectively outside of those confines. I gather that shocks you slightly, Mr. N.? . . .

On any analysis of the above material I think the following is a reasonably accurate summary: society is only being protected to any extent during those periods when the physical limitations of a custodial environment have precluded the accused from engaging in further offences. . . . It is apparent periods of incarceration have not in any way deterred him from further criminal activities, and it is difficult, if not impossible, to assess to what, if any, extent these sentences have acted to deter others. And lastly, it is obvious the reformation or rehabilitation of the accused has not been effected.

Before this Court stands a fifty-year-old man, unskilled, [with] the equivalent of a Grade Six education, no roots in any community, on the lower end of what anyone must regard as the social and economic scale, and, by virtue of poor health, capable of performing only the most menial tasks. Given these details, the Court must attempt to make a judicial application of the principles of protection of society, deterrence, reformation and rehabilitation. . . .

It would be interesting if one could make a comparison between the actual monetary loss incurred by individuals — and I might add that is one of the reasons I requested Mr. B.'s [the victim's] presence this morning — within our society as a result of the criminal activities of the accused, and the monetary loss to society in general as a result of the periods of incarceration of the accused over the past thirty-eight years. . . .

At the present time, as I recall, the actual cost per inmate per year of incarceration in a federal institution is now approximately $13,400 per year. Given the population of Bancroft of roughly 2,500 . . .this means that for each and every year the accused is incarcerated, it will cost, and I emphasize the word "cost," every man, woman, and child approximately five dollars, and I am referring of course to the population of Bancroft. To put it bluntly, society has a vested interest in assuring you are deterred from further criminal activities, and that your reformation and rehabilitation within that society is achieved.

Recognizing several factors, such as the failure of periods of incarceration to achieve the objectives of sentencing, the degree to which you have become institutionalized as a result of such incarceration, and recognizing the factor of the practical matter of cost of incarceration and the concomitant vested interest of society, this Court has decided to adopt an entirely different approach. To put it bluntly, it is this Court's intention to substitute the Village of Bancroft for the physical confines of a prison; the members of society [for] your custodial officers; and the terms of a probation order [for] the formalized rules of the institution. . . . In effect you are being subjected to further institutionalization, albeit within the community; a community which I might add, if success is achieved, has effected a considerable monetary saving, as well as having contributed to your rehabilitation.

To achieve these objectives, the following sentence will be imposed. Sentence will be suspended, and I would point out, Mr. N., I emphasize the word "suspended"; it will have a profound effect on your performance, which I will enunciate later. And you will be placed on probation for a period of three years, and during that period will be bound by the following terms of a probation order:

"(1) you will keep the peace and be of good behaviour. If you commit a further offence you will have breached the terms of the order and the effect of breaching the terms of this order, sir, will be perfectly apparent later.

"(2) you will report to a probation officer on October 1, next, and bi-weekly thereafter at such time and places as he may designate in writing, or as he may require;

"(3) you will remain within the confines of the Village of Bancroft . . . and with one exception will not leave that area without the written approval of your probation officer;

"(4) you will notify the Court, or your probation officer, of any change of address within the municipality of Bancroft;

"(5) you will abstain from the consumption of alcohol absolutely, with one exception, to which I shall later refer; . . .

"(6) you will remain within the jurisdiction of the Court."

Broadly speaking the above conditions establish the physical limitations to which you shall be subjected; the following prescribe in detail the formalized and regularized conduct to which you shall adhere. . . .

"(7) Mondays to Fridays inclusive, of each and every week, you shall comply with the following:

(a) 7:00 A.M., you will get out of bed;

(b) 8:00 A.M., you will report at the Bancroft Ontario Provincial Police Detachment;

(c) 9:00 A.M., you will arrive at W.'s Hardware, Bridge Street;"

Do you know where that is?

MR. N.: Yes, Your Honour.

HIS HONOUR:

"(d) 9:00 A.M. to 12:00 noon, you will commence walking from the last-mentioned point, namely W.'s Hardware, east along the south side of Bridge Street, thence north on Hastings Street to Snow Street on the east side; then the reverse direction to the point of commencement on the opposite side of the street. As you will walk, you will pick up any refuse that may have accumulated since the previous day."

And I trust this will be in co-operation with the Bancroft Department of Public Works.

If the reasons for this last clause are not apparent, I think it would be advantageous to enunciate them. Broadly speaking it coincides with the exercise program to which you would be subjected to in a penal institution; it regularizes your conduct during the morning hours; it recognizes your physical limitations to engage in manual work; it provides you ample time to perform the tasks prescribed, and flexibility to the extent that the regularization of your conduct, and hopefully consequent familiarization with other members of society, may motivate them to request, and you to perform, minor services gratuitously for them. Such familiarity may in part be an answer to the loneliness indicated in the pre-sentence report. And last, but certainly not least, you will be providing a worthwhile service to the community. I might add, I had occasion to drive over that route this morning, and inspect it quite thoroughly, and I am sure you will find ample things to occupy your time for that three-hour period.

This Court is not unmindful of the menial, and what may be regarded by some as demeaning, tasks which have been prescribed. Unfortunately, this Court is restricted, from a practical point of view, to those areas where gratuitous labour can be directed. Hopefully, with community awareness of what this Court is attempting to achieve, suggestions and acceptance will be forthcoming, and this Court will certainly entertain proposals for changes in this term, directing your efforts to other forms of employment. I might add that the Probation Officer for this area very graciously attended here this morning, and I suggest you co-operate with him to a great extent.

"(e) 12:30 P.M., you will attend at your residence;
(f) 12:30 P.M. to 1:30 P.M., lunch at your residence; . . .
(g) 1:30 P.M. to 2:00 P.M., free time at your residence; . . .
(h) 2:00 P.M. to 2:30 P.M., you would walk to the library;
(i) 2:30 P.M. to 4:00 P.M., you would attend at the library;"
. . . This term hopefully achieves two things: one, it regularizes your conduct; secondly, it recognizes the degree of your formal education. Hopefully, subjection to what can only be regarded as an academic atmosphere may engender some self-motivation on your part to either further your education, or to develop skills whereby you would be better prepared to cope with an extremely complex society. . . .

"(j) 4:30 P.M., once more report to the Bancroft Detachment of the Ontario Provincial Police;
(k) 4:30 to 5:30 P.M., free time in the community;
(l) 5:30 P.M. to 6:00 P.M., return home;
(m) 6:00 P.M. to 11:00 P.M., at your residence;
(n) 11:00 P.M., bedtime. . . .
(o) 11:00 P.M. to 7:45 A.M. the following day, in your residence.
"(8) Saturday. Saturday is a different day than Monday to Friday:
(a) 9:00 A.M., report to Bancroft Detachment Ontario Provincial Police;

(b) 9:00 A.M. to 12:00 noon, you will phone the victim and if he is available, as you will perform, and I appreciate his assistance in this regard, you will perform whatever menial tasks he may have available at his residence or such other place as he may direct;"

He was the person who was inconvenienced as a result of your activities and that is why I had him here.

"(c) 12:00 noon to 1:00 P.M., lunch at your residence;
 (d) 1:00 P.M. to 3:00 P.M., you will remain within your residence;
 (e) 3:00 P.M. to 5:00 P.M., shopping in Bancroft, if necessary."

Now, as indicated earlier, Mr. N., you are prohibited from consuming alcohol absolutely; however, there is one exception. That exception is that you may purchase and consume six bottles of beer, such purchase to be made between the hours of 3:00 and 5:00 P.M. on Saturday afternoon, and forthwith thereafter taken directly to your residence. That means there is no [hard] liquor. . . .

"(f) 5:00 P.M., report to Bancroft Detachment Ontario Provincial Police;
 (g) 5:00 P.M. to 11:00 P.M., dinner, and attendance at your residence."

During these hours you may attend any social function or theatre within Bancroft. However before so doing on any Saturday evening, you will advise the Ontario Provincial Police, Bancroft Detachment, of the place where you can be located and the time of your proposed attendance. . . .

"(h) 11:00 P.M., bedtime.
"(9) Sunday:
 (a) To 10:00 A.M., at your residence;
 (b) 10:30 A.M., report Bancroft Detachment Ontario Provincial Police;
 (c) 11:00 A.M. —"

What church do you attend, Mr. N.?

MR. N.: Well I haven't been going to church around here, Your Honour.

HIS HONOUR: You are going to attend church. Do you have any preference?

MR. N.: United Church, Your Honour.

HIS HONOUR: United Church? Well, I seriously entertained the possibility of you attending a Protestant church on Sunday and a Catholic church the next Sunday, but I will restrict it to the United Church, if that is the one you wish to attend, sir.

"You will attend the United Church at 11:00 A.M."

The intention of this requirement is to once more regularize your conduct in the community. Do you see the pattern, Mr. N.? At every given moment of the day someone can tell exactly where you are supposed to be, exactly the same way as a custodial officer in the Kingston Penitentiary. Hopefully it may engender discourse and

involvement in community affairs which will assist in your
rehabilitation.

      "(d) 1:00 P.M. to 2:00 P.M., lunch at your residence;
       (e) 2:00 P.M. to 5:00 P.M., during this period you may, if you so
           desire, attend at your mother's residence;"

This of course is the only situation in which you are permitted to
depart from the Village of Bancroft. As a pre-condition to attendance
at your mother's residence, you are to advise the Ontario Provincial
Police at the morning reporting time of your intention so to attend.
That means when you attend at the Provincial Police at 10:30 on
Sunday morning and you intend that afternoon to go to your mother's
residence, you will advise that office of that intention, sir.

       "(f) 5:00 P.M., report to Bancroft Detachment Ontario
           Provincial Police;
       (g) 5:30 P.M. at your residence from then until the Monday
           schedule commences. . . ."

I well recognize that for this sentence to achieve any degree of
success, it requires the co-operation of not only yourself, but the
Court, your Probation Officers, police officers, and last, but certainly
not least, the community itself. If your rehabilitation can be effected, I
am sure all persons concerned will be extremely gratified, to say the
least, by being in a position to say they contributed in some small way
to the recapture of a member of our society who has finally reached the
stage of being branded a "burnt-out recidivist."

Mr. N., I did not write it out, but I can tell you this Court is not
naive. It may appear to be at first glance, but I would point out to you,
sir, . . . the onus is on you to comply with the terms of this order.
Sentence has been suspended. If you breach any of the terms of this
order you can be brought back before this Court and sentenced for
this offence. I imposed a three-year probation order, because I was
entertaining a three-year period of incarceration in a penitentiary. The
choice is yours as to whether this is effective. . . .

I trust, Mr. Counsel, my comments are perfectly apparent. If this
order is not followed, the alternative is a period of incarceration, and
within the limits of a ten year maximum penalty, it will probably
involve a penitentiary term, the cost to the community being, of
course, $13,400 per year.

Aftermath

Judge Clendenning did what he could. He handed down his
sentence, and then left to carry out other judicial duties. It was not his
function to check on the progress of Mr. N.'s probation. The printed
public report ends with the judge's sentence. Indeed, it must be said
that even the sentence report would not have been made generally

available but for a Law Reform Commission study. From the view of the community, however, the essential question is, What happened to Mr. N.? Who knew, and who cared?

Four years after the sentence the only group in the community that really remembers, and, it can be added, cares about, Mr. N. is the police. On balance, they liked the sentence handed down by the judge. "It made a lot of sense," said a corporal with the Ontario Provincial Police detachment in the Village of Bancroft. "We thought that maybe he would have a chance to pull himself out of a bad situation."

For more than a year following sentence Mr. N. did what was required. He kept to the routine set down by the judge. He worked the city streets, reported to the police, visited the library, and developed a social life. He met and began to live with a woman; the police knew of this and said nothing. All went well until the relationship ended and the woman left. Shortly after this, Mr. N. ran away from the community. The police have a warrant for his arrest; they want to question him concerning a break-in and the theft of a small sum of money.

Said one police officer: "We think that he has gone West. We don't know where. It's really a shame. He was doing so well, and basically he is a nice chap."

The police do not consider the experiment in sentencing a failure. For more than a year Mr. N. was not in trouble. He was even an asset to the community. More to the point, the same kind of sentence, applied to others, has been effective.

What would have been the result if some one person had reached Mr. N. at the time his relationship with the woman ended? This was a time of personal stress; it was a time when Mr. N. needed strong support. It was not that people were against him; it was just that there weren't people actively working in his corner, ready and willing to help. So Mr. N. ran.

Could the experiment in community sentencing work in the large city? Does the size and consequent anonymity of the city make the accused a lost person? We think not. On balance people do not live in the whole city; they live in a neighbourhood. In many respects even the largest of cities can be seen as a grouping of small towns, not unlike the Village of Bancroft. With some effort it is possible to find many of the elements of "community" in a place like Toronto, or Vancouver, or Edmonton, or Montreal. And in finding that community, it is also possible to give the accused, perhaps for the first time, a sense of self.

The experiment relating to Mr. N. was not a failure. It was a humane effort which should be repeated many times over. With additional personal support, it probably should be repeated on Mr. N. if he is found and once again brought before the bar of justice.

CHAPTER
SEVEN

The Young: A Different Approach?

Laura . . . has committed no crime, but she will be confined for an indeterminate period of time. She will be given no statutory time off for good behaviour. The fact is her mother does not want Laura to live at home. She wants Laura institutionalized, and she has succeeded in using the juvenile court to achieve her end.

Delinquency, Not Crime

The judge, the police and, to a much more limited extent, the Crown were the community representatives in the sentencing of Mr. N. The victim and a probation officer attended the sentencing. But neither played any real part. The accused was to call the victim regularly and ask if there were chores to do. Indications are that the victim chose not to be involved with the accused. The probation officer did what he could, but, after all, there were so many other cases to handle. Only a limited amount of time could be given to Mr. N.

The judge clearly intended the community to be involved in the sentence handed down. But both as individual citizens and as organized groups the citizens of the Village of Bancroft chose *not* to be directly involved in the life of Mr. N.

The question then arises of the meaning and feasibility of community sentencing. *Does the community really care about persons such as Mr. N.?* Or does it prefer to pay the high cost of custodial care, five dollars per person each year, just to get Mr. N. off the streets, out of sight and out of mind? Can there be any doubt that without community support a weak person like Mr. N., who sees himself as a "loser," is likely to repeat the cycle of crime, conviction, sentence, release and crime?

Remember that Mr. N. did not begin his relationship with the police as an adult. His first contact came as a child. Why wasn't a concerted effort to help him begun at that time? The juvenile law, reflecting community values, is designed to help restore the young person to the community, not to punish him for committing a crime. In its wording, the law governing youthful offenders is humane; it promises corrective action in the interest of the child. Toward that end, the resources of the community are brought to bear.

The Juvenile Delinquents Act provides: "Where a child is adjudged to have committed a delinquency he shall be dealt with, not as an offender, but as one in a condition of delinquency and therefore requiring help and guidance and proper supervision."

At the same time that Mr. N. was being sentenced for his most recent offence, two youths were being brought before the juvenile court. Their stories are different, but they both illustrate the scope of the juvenile court.

Rocco was fifteen years old. For a year he had worked as a delivery person for the Renaldi Fruit Market. Then he was fired. Mrs. Renaldi had found that Rocco had changed some of the C.O.D. bills and pocketed the difference. Nothing was said to the police at the time. Mrs. Renaldi thought that the firing might teach the boy a lesson.

She was wrong. One night, not long after Rocco had been fired, Mrs. Renaldi, resting in her apartment above the store, heard noises below. Her husband investigated and found Rocco with three of his friends. They ran from the store. Mr. Renaldi would just as soon not have called the police, but his wife insisted. She wanted the boys found, tried, and convicted.

The police visited Rocco's home and questioned him in front of his parents. Rocco was ordered to appear in juvenile court. His parents were given a rather full written explanation of the charges. (Whether they understood the charges is another matter.) Rocco was accused of breaking and entering, and charged with being a juvenile delinquent.

At the trial which followed, no Crown attorney appeared. Instead, a police officer stood and gave evidence; he, in effect, served as the Crown. He did not want to do this, but there was no choice. The Minister had long ago decided that juvenile court did not rank at the same level as the regular criminal courts. In the result, Mr. N., an adult offender, faced a Crown attorney who wanted to be sure that the sentence meted out served the interest of the community. Rocco faced a police officer and a judge.

Rocco had counsel available to him. Indeed, if money were a problem, Duty Counsel from the Law Society would ensure that the procedures for free counsel were initiated. In this case, however, there was no fear of being institutionalized. There was every chance that Rocco would be warned and freed. It came as no small surprise to him when the judge ordered him to repay those whom he had robbed. Over a period of time, as a condition of parole, Rocco was to raise the forty dollars which he had taken and turn that money over to the Renaldis.

Rocco did what was required. The police hoped the offence would not be repeated. But they now know Rocco, and they wonder whether this fifteen-year-old will go "straight."

The police could have acted before Rocco ever committed an offence. The law allows a minor to be declared a delinquent for violation of any federal, provincial or municipal law. Furthermore, the law allows for a finding of delinquency if there has been "sexual immorality or any similar form of vice."

The law can be used by parents and schools to rid themselves of children they cannot otherwise control. The law also allows parents and schools to control children who do not want to be subject to their discipline.

As an example, consider the story of Laura. Laura was fourteen years old and lived with her mother. Since the age of eleven, Laura and her mother, Mrs. Hubard, had been unable to get along. Fights were frequent, and Laura was defiant and rebellious. At the age of thirteen she was sexually active and, in her mother's view, even promiscuous. Her mother first went to social service agencies, but in her words "got nowhere." Mrs. Hubard wanted Laura out of the home and under someone else's control. In the end she went to juvenile court. Laura was declared a juvenile delinquent because of her sexual activity and her truancy from school and was committed to a group home located in a suburban neighbourhood. She was to live there with five other youngsters under the supervision of two "house parents" — in the home where Laura was sent, two social workers who lived on the premises. Laura was to participate in the household chores, do shopping at nearby stores, take care of her own room, and interact not only with those who lived in the home but also with neighbours and schoolmates. Her mother was delighted. She had succeeded in putting distance between herself and her difficult daughter while at the same time feeling no guilt. She could even control telephone calls from Laura:

MRS. H.: . . . I told the probation officer: Laura, when she was in the other home, she was calling me three and four and five times a day. She would get me upset, I would end up crying about it, so I told the probation officer the other day. I said, "I don't want Laura calling me every day. I know what she will do." He says, "Well, she's going to call you a few names." I says, "No, if she does, I'll hang up on her." He says, "Well, you can't do that!" And I says, "Well, I can!"

I said, "I'm not going to sit here and listen to a fourteen-year-old call me an effing whore and all this kind of thing." I said, "I won't go through that." So he says, "No, but you'll more or less have to play it along." I says, "No, I won't do that, either. I've put up with almost two years of her going on like this." So I says, "I would rather she just get herself straightened out," 'cause they get professional help there, too.

Consider now the difference between Mr. N. and fourteen-year-old Laura. When Mr. N. was sentenced, a firm and clear probation order was written and the police could easily determine if the terms of the probation were being met. And at the end of a given period of time probation for this man with an extended criminal record was to have ended. Indeed, even if an adult offender is arrested, tried and convicted, his stay in prison will be tightly structured, and there will be controls imposed by the government not only over the prisoner but also over his keepers. They will be required to operate within the law.

Will Laura be given the same fair treatment? Unlike Mr. N., she has committed no crime, but she will be confined for an indeterminate period of time. She will be given no statutory time off for good behaviour. The fact is that her mother does not want Laura to live at home. She wants Laura institutionalized, and she has succeeded in using the juvenile court to achieve her end.

"Homes" for the Young

A group home is located in the community. It affords an opportunity to be a part of the community. The functions that are expected of a group home are clear, and worthy of praise. It does not follow, however, that stated functions become living realities.

In 1975, in a then-confidential report, the Ontario government commented on the supervision and standards of group homes.

The judge in each jurisdiction oversees the operation of the facilities. Many of the staff are untrained and inexperienced. Some have had previous experience in child and adult correctional institutions. There are no standards written in the legislation and no guidelines. No one with specific residential care experience is employed by the Ministry to inspect the facilities and this task falls to the Chief Judge, who is unable to give appropriate attention to it, and to the Grand Juries. In general the standards of the Children's Boarding Homes Act are followed.

Why would government allow group homes to be established without standards? The Juvenile Delinquents Act speaks of children in need of protection. To assign children to homes without standards relating to their care can hardly be seen as protecting the young.

The answer is both clear and disturbing: children can be shunted from one institution to another because money is saved, and, in the final result, most of those in the community simply do not care. There are few to shout their objections to government cost-cutting. There are few who speak for the young, and the young are denied the means to speak for themselves.

Let there be no doubt that government acted as it did in the establishment of group homes to save money. The confidential memorandum quoted above commented on the absence of standards in group homes not as part of a review of the *quality* of custodial care, but as part of a review of the *costs* of care. By 1975 the Ontario government had doubled the amount of money budgeted for children's services to $22 million annually. The daily rate per child in some institutions ranged from $59 to $130. The average cost for institutional care for a child was about $50 per day. To maintain a child in a group home cost only $27, a saving of almost half compared with the institutional rate.

The government of Ontario, a wealthy province, opted for cost savings over effective child care and protection. Restoring the child to the community has not been a matter of high priority. Government seems to share the feelings of Laura's mother, who does not want to be bothered by her daughter, who wants her daughter out of sight and out of mind.

In fact, if cost savings were the only force acting on government, then money would not have flowed from institutional homes to group homes. Government money would have been directed to the support of families in stress. As a matter of government policy, assistance would have been provided to Laura and her mother. Specific social services would have been offered to help them either to work through their problems so that they might better live together, or to make the necessary adjustment to live apart.

In 1975, as today, it would have been cheaper to have provided a homemaker and the twice-weekly visits of a social worker, than to have placed a child in a group home.

But the government has not chosen to emphasize home-support programmes, apparently mainly because institutions, whether they are large or small, take the child out of the home, away from the neighborhood, and away from the family. For most of those concerned, that is the easier course.

It was not until September, 1978, that the province of Ontario, which has 800 residences for children, with a total capacity of about

25,000 children, *proposed* a bill of rights for children's residences then loosely licensed. What a curious matter! After several years of operation, supposedly for the protection of children, residences were asked to consider and comment upon their central purpose, their reason for being. In announcing the proposed bill of rights ministry spokesmen noted that the proposals would be seen as controversial.

Now hear the proposals directed to child warehousing facilities. Understand that these "homes" are no longer operated solely by charitable institutions. Today they are also operated by corporations that can make a profit from the daily rate paid to hold a child. This is the proposed bill of rights:

—Every child has the right to access to Ontario's children's residences free from discrimination on the basis of race, religion, or ethnic origin.

—Every child has the right to live in clean, safe surroundings.

—Every child has the right to receive adequate and appropriate food, clothing and housing.

—Every child has the right to receive adequate and appropriate medical care.

—Every child has the right to be free from physical abuse and inhumane treatment.

—Every child has the right to receive appropriate and reasonable adult guidance, support and supervision.

—Every child has the right to receive an educational programme.

—Every child has the right to enjoy freedom of thought and of conscience.

—Every child has the right to the reasonable enjoyment of privacy.

—Every child has the right to have his or her opinions heard and to be included, to the greatest extent possible, when any decisions are being made affecting his or her life.

In support of the proposed rights a grievance procedure would be established. Through it children could voice disagreements and air problems relating to administrative decisions. Moreover, before children could be subjected to treatment they would have to be consulted and their permission obtained so long as they were between the ages of twelve and sixteen.

The proposed system would affect Laura. Depending on the group home to which she was sent Laura may, under the present regimen, be subjected to corporal punishment for disobedience. If Laura were told not to telephone or visit her mother, and she disobeyed, she could, in some homes, be punished with the strap. If the strap failed and Laura continued to "act out," a physician might prescribe a heavy dose of tranquillizers to sedate and control her.

The proposed bill of rights would severely curtail the use of corporal punishment. And the prescribing of tranquillizers as a method of treatment would have to meet with the approval of Laura.

84

The proposed system is seen as a major reform. Yet let us refer again to Mr. N. If he were imprisoned in a Canadian penitentiary, almost all the rights proposed for Laura as a child in need of protection would be his as a matter of course. Mr. N. need not fear being strapped. Nor need he worry about being subjected to medical treatment without his consent. At least on paper, educational programmes are his to chose, and the more he takes advantage of such programmes, the more likely it is that he will qualify for release.

No Homes for Some

In some respects, however, Laura can be seen as lucky. She is in the kind of facility that others want. This is not because Laura's "home" is basically good; it is because this sort of facility is the least bad possibility. In 1975 it was estimated that there were about 71,000 moderately to severely disturbed teenagers in the province of Ontario. Social service agencies were thought to be reaching about half that number. It is out of this group of disturbed children that much of the problem of youth crime evolves.

Laura could be placed in a group home because she was lucky, and because she lives in a large city. Those who live in small towns are less fortunate. Consider the town of Brockville which is served by Juvenile Court Judge John A. Deacon. The court sits on Tuesdays. Duty Counsel has been named to help the children and their families to understand and respond to the charges. But this is what he says: "I know, the kids know, and everybody else knows that most of them are just going to get a slap on the hand. . . . Technically, I don't think they comprehend the big picture. . . . They know the guy up there is a judge, and the guy in uniform is a cop, and they know they've done bad."

View "the big picture" as seen through the eyes of children. See what they see. If the child was kept in custody pending the hearing — and this sometimes does happen — it means the child was held in the Brockville provincial jail. The closest detention home for children is located about a hundred miles away.

The court waiting room can hold only six persons. The overflow, and there is always an overflow, spills into the public corridor. The courtroom itself has a sign stating, CLOSED COURT. This is done to protect the child from public exposure. But Brockville is a town of about 19,000 and, as the children sit in the public corridors, their chance of anonymity is rather remote.

One by one the children are called into the courtroom. The judge acts as his own clerk. He rattles off the charge in the language of the Criminal Code: "You are charged on or about the 15th day of February at Brockville in the United Counties of Leeds and Grenville with committing a delinquency in that you did take a motor vehicle, to wit, a 1965 Buick . . . without the consent of the owner. . . ."

No evidence is heard as to whether the child really understands the charge against him. Nor is evidence heard as to whether the child is in fact guilty in law. The child pleads guilty, but he is not asked to explain either what he did, or, more importantly, why he did it. (It should be noted that about 90 per cent of all juveniles brought before this court and every other juvenile court in Canada do plead guilty.)

The judge can order reports dealing with the child to be prepared by the Children's Aid Society. Michael Valpy, a skilled journalist for the *Toronto Globe and Mail,* wrote of the disposition reports submitted to the judge on one day.

> Judge Deacon relates that reports are prepared on well over 60 per cent of the youngsters found delinquent. . . . They are highly sensitive documents, requiring considerable skill in preparation and purporting to be analyses of not just the child's behaviour but that of his whole family.
>
> The six reports submitted to Judge Deacon on this day are most subjective, making unsupported surmises that psychologists and psychiatrists would hesitate to make. They are heavy with sociological phrasing and contain passages such as: "The father, I am told, is promiscuous" — or they state baldly, on the strength of one or two interviews without backup evidence, that parents have lost control of their children.
>
> Neither of the two [social service] officers who wrote the reports is in court. Only Mr. MacEachern is present to answer questions. He says he has gone over the documents with the authors — meaning that if he says anything in court, it might likely be hearsay about hearsay. . . .
>
> The reports are shown to parents when they turn up with their children for the court session on disposition. With the authors absent, there is no one competent to sit down and go over the material.

Often the parents do not even know what they are reading.

For all the reports that might be written, whatever their quality, there is a limited range of possibilities open to the judge in terms of sentencing. He can place the child on probation. He can order the child to be committed to a training school. Or he can place the child under the control of the Children's Aid Society.

The province's training schools already are overcrowded, and the Children's Aid Society can offer little help. Referral to the Children's Aid Society means placing the child in a foster home — and such homes simply are not available. Most people do not want to take troubled teenagers. If the judge should order three children placed in the care of the Children's Aid Society, there would be an organizational crisis. The Society would have nowhere to put the children.

The judge is aware of the situation. So he does what is necessary. He tends to place children on probation. He hopes that a warning will do the job.

The Front Line: The Police

Watching the proceedings are not only the children and their parents, but also the police, who, more often than not, had laid the charges that brought the children to the court. What they see they do not like. What is the sense of detaining and charging a child who simply goes through a process very much like turnstile justice?

A Toronto juvenile court judge recorded the appearance before him of one girl twenty-eight different times between 1975 and 1978.

The police in more than one community have begun to shape new approaches toward the juvenile. The new approaches seem to assume the limitations of the juvenile law. One big-city police officer stated quite openly that he hesitates to lay charges against a juvenile. As a police officer he has more control over the young when he operates outside the court system.

> It's better to put the fear of God into a kid on the street than have him get into court and have him see what a farce it is. . . . Because after he's been through the courts a couple of times and got off with a *sine die* adjournment, he thinks it's a joke.

But the police do not joke. The young, more often than not, live in the same reality as the police, the reality of the street. Through their power to lay charges the police have been shaping their own judicial system. In eyeball contact with the young and their parents, the police decide whether to lay charges or to move toward another approach which they themselves will supervise. In some cities, including Toronto, police departments have established Youth Bureaus, staffed by officers who may be trained to deal with the young, but who remain, first and most importantly, police officers. To resolve conflicts they do not tend to use other social service agencies. They tend to handle the matter within the department. As a last resort, they may refer the issue to the juvenile court with the view toward having the child institutionalized.

These are officers who speak what they feel. If a child has been caught stealing, they may call him a thief. If the child has been found with a dangerous weapon, then there will be a full personal search, and an examination of the child's file. There is likely to be a firm, even a hard, quality in encounters between the police and the young. In Toronto Constable Jackson read from the contact card of a thirteen-year-old who had thrown a bottle and partially destroyed a neon sign:

"Assault on a seven-year-old, theft, attempted robbery — God, you're a real winner, aren't you? . . . This is getting pretty serious. You could go to training school for this, especially with all the other trouble you've been in."

The thirteen-year-old admits the damage. The constable confers with three other officers. They decide to lay charges. They will make a point of pressing for special sentencing at the hearing.

Yet it is not difficult to find other dispositions for what appears to be the same offence. The following is taken from the records of the Toronto police Youth Bureau: "Willful Damage — April 27, 1974 — Cautioned — Five juveniles. . . . On Thursday, the five boys were caught leaving the underground garage after a number of light bulbs had been smashed. [The superintendant of the building] obtained their names and reported the incident to the police. The parents of all the boys were called today and brought their sons in. All admitted breaking some of the lights. Restitution will be made by each of the boys." No charges were laid. The police conducted their own investigation, made their own findings, and administered their own justice — promptly, efficiently and without use of the courts.

Detailed statistics on the youthful offender are not easy to obtain. Most police departments keep only rough, general figures. The Toronto police force, through its rather sophisticated Youth Bureau, has maintained data more complex than most other departments.

What those statistics indicate is that the police often take the initiative with the young. About 43 per cent of all police contacts with juveniles are not crime-related. That is, the police are only asking questions; they are checking general behaviour.

For the police in Toronto there seem to be only two courses of action with the young: either the matter will be handled by the police themselves through some informal understanding such as restitution, or charges will be laid. Only about one per cent of all matters that come before the police are referred to other social service agencies. The reason is that the police simply are not confident that such agencies as Children's Aid can handle the problems.

Community Judges

In the final analysis, however, the police have only a limited range of discretion. For serious violations of the law the police have no choice but to lay charges. And even with less serious offences, where the police can exercise discretion, there is always the danger that they will overstep their authority. The police are not intended by the community to be judges of the law; that is the function of the court.

Judge W. G. Golden of Muskoka and Chief Rodney Monague of the Christian Island band understand the potential role of the court. They know that the judge need not function in isolation. It is one matter for a judge to pass upon the law; it is quite a different matter for him to hand down the sentence alone, removed from the community.

Christian Island in Ontario is an Indian reserve. About 60 per cent of its five hundred members are under the age of sixteen. Chief Monague is twenty-three years old. Recently the reserve was faced with a rash of vandalism, petty thefts, and break-ins. The crimes were largely the work of the young.

Judge Golden and the tribal Council decided upon a response. Two members of the tribal Council were selected to sit with Judge Golden. They participate actively in deciding, implementing and supervising sentences meted out to the young. The young see no strangers on the bench handing down justice. They see their elders, the leaders of their community. And the sentences which are handed down call for the young to do work — useful work — in their community.

The young are not removed from their community as a result of their delinquency. Rather, they are brought back into the tribe. They see that their elders have more than a passing interest in them.

This is no turnstile justice. This is an attempt to understand the young, and to develop mature band members. The rate of delinquency has dropped significantly. In this example there is much for the larger community to learn.

CHAPTER
EIGHT

Life and Death Choices

The courts presently are not equipped either by temperament or training to handle fundamental issues of justice. The courts cannot and should not alone perform the role best left to the community and the community's voice, the legislature.

Law without Policy: A Story

Paul Helm, age thirty-six, sat at the wheel of his car, on the highway outside his farmhouse. He waited for the oncoming traffic to pass so he could turn left into his driveway. Paul noted that the last car in the approaching line was an old Cadillac. I'll turn after that car, thought Paul as he cranked his wheel over.

The driver of the Cadillac was Laurence Kiley, age sixty-two. Rushing back from his cottage, he was going faster than the speed limit, but he checked to be sure the car stopped to turn left in front of him would wait till he had passed. Kiley knew he had been seen so he accelerated.

At precisely that moment, John Fascall, age seventeen, coming up behind Helms on the other side of the road, turned to the passenger in his car, Ted Orcutt, age eighteen, and said it had been a "great party." John and Ted were both drunk, but John was confident of his driving. Too late John's eyes returned to the road. Too late he realized that the car he was following had stopped to turn left. Too late he jerked the wheel to swerve.

Fascall's car smashed into the rear of Helm's car and ricocheted off the road into a tree. Helm's car spun into the oncoming lane. Kiley had barely time to touch his brake. He struck the side of Helm's car.

Fascall, said the reports, died instantaneously. Orcutt was thrown out of the car, sustaining critical injuries. He was rushed to the hospital

90

where he underwent immediate surgery. Laurence Kiley was rushed to the hospital but was pronounced dead on arrival. Helm was rushed to surgery as well.

Young Orcutt came out of the operating room alive, but in a deep coma. The doctors were sure that if he survived he would, judging from the head injuries he had sustained, be physically handicapped and certainly mentally retarded for the rest of his life. Soon Orcutt showed signs of having developed pneumonia. The condition might well kill him. His doctors had to decide whether to give full effort to defeating the pneumonia, or to allow Orcutt to die mercifully.

But on what basis should the doctors make such a decision? Should they advise Orcutt's parents of the situation and allow them to make the decision? Could the Orcutts make a sound choice in the midst of this catastrophe? What if they later feel that they had decided wrongly, or that the doctors had guided them to one answer or the other?

The doctors' primary concern must be with their duty as spelled out by their ethics and the law. They have sworn an oath to preserve life. The law charges them with the same responsibility. The doctors may make a choice that it would be better for Orcutt to die, and let him die. But then they must face the possibility that the Orcutts might charge them with malpractice, or that the Crown could charge them with murder under the criminal law.

The decision as to whether this boy will live or die may depend on a series of particular circumstances. What are the doctors' personal beliefs? How long have they known the parents? Are the parents likely to sue? Will the subject ever be made public? Indeed the crucial question, What is best for the patient?, may not be the most important factor in the decision.

But should such a decision be in the hands of doctors or parents? Is this not a question that affects all of society?

Any one of us might be in Orcutt's position. Do we want to have the decision of whether we live or die in the hands of a doctor? That seems to be the reason that doctors are now not given much of a choice. There is a section in the Criminal Code of Canada which prohibits the withholding of treatment if that would cause the patient's death. Society seems to have spoken through the legislature and the courts to say that a doctor must do everything to save the patient's life. The ruling seems clear enough.

But what of someone like Paul Helm? He was critically injured and underwent surgery, hooked up to machines that kept his body alive through the operation. The surgery was a "success"; his body is alive. But after the operation he could not be taken off the machine. The machine was literally keeping him alive. But Paul Helm doesn't know that, because Paul Helm has a brain that shows no activity. In the doctor's words, Paul is "brain dead."

Paul is lying on a bed, his body attached by tubes and cords to a machine plugged into a simple wall socket. If the power were to go off, he would no longer have a beating heart or breathing lungs. But that won't happen. The hospital has an emergency auxiliary power unit. So Paul may lie there for hours, months, years — no one knows how long. And all the time he is there the flat line on a small, green screen will show the inactivity of his lifeless brain.

Paul's doctor is Jo-Anne Birch, M.D. She believes that Paul is dead. Medically she *knows* that he is dead. But Dr. Birch knows that others would say that where a heart beats there is yet life. Dr. Birch is positive there is no chance that Paul will ever be anything other than what he now is. The situation is desperate for Paul's family. The man is neither dead nor alive. They are torn between their hope for a miraculous recovery and their knowledge that the present situation could continue not just for days but for years. Furthermore, it is expensive both to the state, which pays most of the medical bills, and to the family which has lost its breadwinner as surely as though he were dead. Financially the family is in limbo: they cannot collect on any of the life insurance Paul so carefully purchased.

Consider the plight of Dr. Birch. Morally convinced that Paul is medically dead and wishing to end the agony for his family, she would like to "pull the plug." She is strengthened in her conviction by a document which she has in her possession. It reads:

> I, Paul Franklin Helm, now being of sound mind and good health, write the following directions to my physician.
>   (1) Should accident or illness or a combination thereof ever cause me to become so ill that my body can only be kept alive by mechanical means
> AND
>   (2) It is your corroborated opinion that my brain is so dramatically impaired as to be "brain dead"
> THEN
>   (3) Twenty-four hours after brain activity has ceased — all medical and mechanical support is to be withdrawn.
>   (4) I thus remove permission for medical attention if my brain should cease to function.
>   (5) You may take such organs as may be useful for transplant purposes.
>   (6) In so instructing you, my physician, it is to be understood that I am *not* asking you to aid in my suicide. Such an act would not be causing my death. If my brain dies, I am dead. In so requesting I am merely asserting my right to die naturally — body and brain dying simultaneously as intended.
> Signed, witnessed and dated.

Doesn't that solve Dr. Birch's dilemma? Far from it. The document is not legally binding; there is no law that allows a person to determine the criterion for his or her own death. Society has expressed its disapproval for suicide through the Criminal Code.

Suppose that Dr. Birch followed her conscience and disconnected the life support apparatus. Paul's heart stops. He is now pronounced (by a doctor) to be dead.

What is the state then to do? Literally, Paul has been killed. Who should be charged with his homicide? Should the Crown charge Dr. Birch who apparently has violated Section 209 of the Canadian Criminal Code? She surely has accelerated the time of Paul's death. Should the Crown charge Orcutt as being party to the death? After all, he helped a minor purchase liquor and allowed him to drive while impaired. Does the fault lie with Laurence Kiley, who was speeding? If he had been travelling at the speed limit he might have avoided the accident. Does the fault lie with Fascall who drove with what might be described as criminal negligence? Or does the state say that Paul Helm committed suicide, but Dr. Birch is guilty of aiding and abetting that suicide?

Society has rendered its judgements on most of these questions. There is a small penalty for selling liquor to a minor. Driving while impaired carries a penalty. Killing someone by reckless driving can earn a life sentence in prison. But Dr. Birch, who clearly had the least to do with Paul's death, can be charged with culpable homicide, the most serious of the charges. That is largely because society has not spoken on the issue of what is actual death, and on the power of people to instruct physicians *not* to save their lives.

Perhaps if Dr. Birch were charged society would have the opportunity of deciding this important issue. Certainly the fate of Dr. Birch would influence the actions of other doctors. Yet would it be fair to place Dr. Birch in prison if the court decided that a mechanically induced heartbeat constituted life?

Public Policy: Defining the Criminal Law

The courtroom seems an unlikely place to decide what is life and what is death. Surely that is the province of the citizenry properly informed. In fact, although the court will pass upon the action of Dr. Birch, it is not deciding what is life or death. It is rendering a narrow legal interpretation from which flows important consequences. The court is deciding what the legislature meant when it wrote the word "death" into the Criminal Code. The court, following arcane rules, attempts to understand the expression of Parliament, a community of elected officials who, it is presumed, speak for the larger community.

The way the court decides this is by listening to lawyers argue previous court cases dealing with the same question, the dictionary meaning of words, and their application to facts.

The court's search for meaning seldom is a quest for values. Precedent relates to the past, not the future. It deals with cases and facts that may have little real application to the fundamental value choices that the community expects will be resolved in trial. There is a false assumption that courts are concerned with abstract justice. They are not; they are concerned with the interpretation and application of law. The courts presently are not equipped either by temperament or training to handle fundamental issues of justice. The courts cannot and should not alone perform the role best left to the community and the community's voice, the legislature.

Nor can the task of shaping values be left to experts, to physicians for example. It is one matter for physicians to describe the medical facts of "brain death," and the likelihood of recovery. It is quite another matter for any doctor to take a personal decision, without the sanction of the community, that would terminate life.

It is through the legislature that principles of law can and should be stated. There the hard decisions are made, not only on the dramatic questions of life and death but also on matters of routine that heavily influence the workings of the criminal justice system — matters like the definition of crimes, the rules for sentencing, imprisonment, diversion and the use of the police.

There is an assumption in the public mind that such issues need not be explicitly stated or openly debated. There is a feeling that matters will be sorted out in the proper way. In the matter of "brain death" for instance:

> We tend to assume that such dilemmas will be solved by a common sense approach, such as "no physician would ever be prosecuted for such an act." However, this is small comfort to the physician who has been prosecuted, if the common sense of a Crown attorney led to the conclusion that "no physician would ever remove such an apparatus from a person who was legally alive." In addition, of course, such an open-ended approach may not be appropriate if the law is to continue to furnish effective protection for human life in a way that is consistent with the physician's duty in an age of rapid development of medical technology.
>
> The rules that apply to this situation, in Fuller's words, simply "shout their contradictions across the vacuum." Ethics, morals, law, hospital policy, Crown discretion, the physician's concept of duty and the patient's claim to life all compete for pre-eminence. The law, as the ultimate arbiter of the policy preferences of the society, must eventually decide the issues posed by these facts. . . . Where present rules fall

short, however, the solution to the problem must be sought in the inquiry, "What values are we trying to protect and why?"

The fundamentals of our criminal law require ongoing political examination. Legislators and, more importantly, the electorate, must have the will and the courage to make choices. If nothing is done the criminal law simply stands and is enforced. Crimes remain the crimes defined in years past. The system remains the system used over the decades. The festering continues, only occasionally pricked by the moral dilemma of a Dr. Birch.

What is meant by community discussion and decision? Take the matter of capital punishment. On balance, it probably can be said that the voters favour some form of capital punishment. Yet the legislature has refused to follow the popular will. Does this mean that the view of the electorate has no meaning? No. The legislature was elected not to mirror the popular will, but to govern, with the opportunity, from time to time, for the electorate to make choices. In no way does the will of the legislature expressed through its condemnation of capital punishment demonstrate either the absence of representative democracy or a failure to listen. In the final analysis, if the electorate does not like the decision, there is a remedy at the ballot box.

Another example: The government believes that the general will is against abortion. Thus the Criminal Code provides strict limitations on abortion. (There must be three doctors who agree that it is necessary to preserve the health of the mother. The decision is made by a hospital committee which permits abortions.)

Dr. Henry Morgentaler challenged this provision. He believed the law permitted him to act independently. He believed that he was bound by the duty imposed by the Criminal Code to provide medical service to those in need. He said that the Criminal Code, Section 45, permitted a doctor to perform an operation if it was "reasonable in all circumstances." He said that, in all the circumstances, the abortion he gave to a nineteen-year-old immigrant was reasonable. The Crown did not agree. He was charged with committing a criminal offence and held in prison.

Dr. Morgentaler's case went to court and to the people. It aroused heated debate throughout Canada. Thousands wrote petitions, contributed monies to his defense fund and urged the cause before influential persons.

The case went to the courts. Morgentaler was tried by judge and jury. In a sense the jury is the community's voice in criminal matters. It alone is primarily charged with finding the facts. The role of the judge is to find the law, and instruct the jury accordingly. The jury in the Morgentaler case said that he may have broken the letter of the law, but he was no criminal. They said that it was wrong to call this man a threat to society. The community had spoken by declaring that the abortion for which Morgentaler was charged was reasonable in all the circumstances.

The state, which had pressed the charges, was not prepared to accept the verdict of the community. It appealed the decision of the court. The appeal succeeded. To the appellate court the jury had clearly ignored the law in arriving at its findings of fact. The judges said that Section 45 of the Criminal Code, allowing for reasonable justification, was no defence for an abortion offence. Morgentaler must be guilty. The appeal court substituted a conviction, and Morgentaler was jailed.

The system of criminal justice was distorted. Here an individual was jailed after being acquitted by a jury. The appellate court did not order a new trial; instead it put itself in the place of the jury and substituted its judgment for that of Morgentaler's peers. And the Supreme Court of Canada upheld the action of the Quebec Appeal Court.

But the community would not be stilled. Morgentaler, the individual, became Morgentaler, the cause. The electorate forced Parliament to act. The legislature passed a law saying an appeal court could not convict where a jury had acquitted. Morgentaler was freed. But the question remains: Is the court a place for the resolution of moral issues? The answer seems clear. The court functions in a narrow setting; it is not the arbiter of fundamental values. The court works on rules and precedent. It reaches rulings on particular cases. It does not claim to express the community will. At best, and then only at the time of sentence, the court can temper the words of the law to fit individual circumstance. On balance, the criminal justice system as implemented in the courts is a highly technical and ritualized system. In the finding of guilt the court is not creative or sensitive.

Making Moral Decisions

Yet the court must make moral decisions. In effect the court expresses, through the use of powerful sanctions, society's approval or disapproval of certain types of conduct. The difficulty is that the court is placed in the position of being a moral authority without discretion. It must act in accordance with the laws passed by Parliament. It must find guilt or innocence in accord with stated law. This means that the Parliament is the moral determiner. And Parliament acts only in general terms; it cannot deal easily with the specific facts in an individual case which might cry out for a finding of innocence. Parliament cannot easily deal with a Dr. Birch or a Dr. Morgentaler. And, in the result, neither can the courts. The effect is a moral void.

The potential dangers of such a situation are many. Chief among them is the alienation of the responsibility for criminal justice from the community. The people who staff the criminal justice system are not thought of as part of the community but rather as servants of the government. As the public grows more and more isolated from its responsibilities, the more isolated become the men and women who staff the system. They see that what they do is a specialty. They are stuck with some of society's dirty work because that is what they are paid to do. No longer are they doing what is every citizen's responsibility; they are doing what most will not.

Is it any wonder that those actively dealing with crime and criminals can only treat it as a job? Society has declared that it is some other person's task. The courts only illustrate the flaw which pervades every segment of the criminal justice system. The law is declared without flexibility. Only in the nuances of interpretation or in the discretion in sentencing can justice as a real concept be reached and applied.

The courts are denied the opportunity to do what the community expects. The courts cannot deal with justice directly, openly, critically.

The fundamental duty of the criminal justice system is to render justice. This should be a mandate imposed not only on the courts but on all the constituent parts of the system. Let there be no mistake: justice does have meaning. It is the active process of preventing injustice and wrong. It is not the rigid, ritualistic interpretation of law by mysterious ways. It is not the police acting secretly. It is not a prison system, operating by private rules, hidden away from the community. Justice, the prevention of wrong-doing, must involve all of the community.

Edmond Cahn wrote:

> Justice, as we shall use the term, means the active process of remedying
> or preventing what would arouse the sense of injustice. . . . Whatever
> its pragmatic limitations, the judicial process is required to exhibit fair
> effort at finding truth and exercising wisdom. Without that effort —
> involving notice, hearing, and deliberation — it loses its rank as
> process; it becomes gross will.

It is both freedom and responsibility under the law which must be extended to the courts, the police, correctional authorities and, finally, to the community. This is not a sterile abstraction. It is a concept that finds its vitality in life and to which those who administer it are responsible.

Denied the freedom to prevent injustice, all elements of the criminal justice system suffer. Roles become jobs of only limited responsibility; discretion of a secret kind is exercised. Individual success rather than community involvement becomes the standard for all.

For the police in a para-military organization this means following orders and doing the specific task assigned. For the Crown prosecutor it means "handling the case load," maintaining efficiency and processing the accused.

For the judge it means following the law, ensuring that the statutes of the government are carefully observed. For the prison guard it is making sure no one escapes and no guard is wounded or killed.

For all these men and women, two facts are certain: society does not appreciate what they do, and the overall task — anything beyond their day-to-day tasks — seems hopeless. It is ludicrous for the Crown to talk about "justice" when there must be plea bargaining just to keep the delay in handling cases down to a few months.

Justice is no cloistered virtue. It demands the scrutiny and the respectful, even if outspoken, comments of ordinary people. The challenge is one of involvement. The criminal justice system must not be allowed to slip into the hands of so-called experts. There must be involvement because the liberty and safety of the community are affected. There must be involvement for the sake of those who staff the system. They must not be removed from the citizenry; they must have the legitimacy of being a part of the community.

As Edmond Cahn said of capital punishment:

> We who live as free citizens in a democratic society are responsible for capital punishment imposed by our law. Every day the penal codes draw their validity from our name, the executions are ordered by our authority, and the rope or electric current or lethal gas is bought with our tax money. There is no one else: it is we who arrange, through hired deputies, for pulling the lever or pressing the button.

What Cahn said of capital punishment applies to every aspect of the criminal justice system. Capital punishment is the single act of ending a life. There is also the far worse punishment of taking a life slowly, day by day, month by month, and year by year that tears at and corrupts the prisoner, the police, the Crown, the judge and the jailer.

NOTES
Chapter One

False, Unreasoning Fear: A Fortress Mentality

In a study extending over several years and involving numerous "working papers" as well as reports, the Law Reform Commission of Canada tried to grapple with the subject of crime and the law. With uncommon effort for a government funded agency the Law Reform Commission sought communication and dialogue with the citizenry as well as the academic community. A culminating report, titled *Our Criminal Law*, was published in March 1976 (Ottawa: Information Canada). What the Law Reform Commission said was backed by detailed data. Some of its conclusions deserve to be repeated.

Expectations

Expectations are maybe to blame. We expect the law to protect us and reduce the volume of crime, yet, as we know, the vast majority of crimes are not cleared up. For every crime prosecuted there may be ten reported and forty unreported. Reducing this "dark number" of crime would need more police, better equipment, greater willingness to report incidents and to help the authorities, and also a very different criminal law. The kind of law we have can never guarantee protection — in general it only moves in *after* the event and bolts the door after the horse has escaped. Our criminal law looks to the past. Protection comes from looking to the future. [p. 2]

Reality

Next, take the operation of the criminal justice system. In theory the law aims to promote humanity. In practice it is frequently itself inhuman. Canada, it has been shown, is one of the harshest Western countries when it comes to use of prison sentences. Many of the terms imposed are far too long, half the people in prison should never be there, and so many are in gaol that those few needing real care and attention cannot get it. Indeed the whole system resembles a vast machine sucking people in one end, spewing them out the other and then sucking them back in again — a self-generating mechanism, certainly not a human process. . . .

Or take the presumption of innocence. Again, in theory the prosecution must prove guilt. In reality the defendant often fights under a handicap — appearances, his clothes, his way of speaking, his very presence in the dock, all tell against him.

Finally, the principle of justice. Here again reality falls short of aspiration. In theory crimes are crimes and punished equally no matter who commits them. In practice the penalty often depends, not on the nature of the crime, but on the person who commits it. Our prison population, for example, contains a quite unrepresentative proportion of poor, of disadvantaged and of native offenders. The richer you are, the better your chance of getting away with something. Is it that rich men make the laws and so what rich men do is not a crime but simply shrewd business practice? Or is it that position and wealth protect the rich against intervention? Certainly more poor than rich are prosecuted even on a proportional reckoning. Or is it that those who can afford expensive lawyers have a better hope of being acquited? For all the respect we pay to justice and equality, we still have one law for the rich and another for the poor.

Worst of all, our picture of the criminal justice system bears little resemblance to reality. Supposedly it is a system designed to try defendants, assess their criminal liability on the evidence and determine the proper penalty in the light of all the circumstances; in real life trials are a comparative rarity, the vast majority of defendants plead guilty and the real work of the system takes place behind closed doors, between the crown attorney and the defendant's lawyer at the plea-bargaining table. Theoretically we demonstrate our public disapproval of certain types of conduct; in practice all we do is process an interminable series of recurring cases along the dreary assembly line of dime-store justice. Judges, crown attorneys, defence lawyers, police and all concerned in the operation of the system grow daily more disillusioned and discouraged. Small wonder many think our criminal law a hollow mockery. [pp. 11-13]

There is difficulty in obtaining either precise crime statistics or those that give a composite profile of law enforcement agencies. In April, 1978, Statistics Canada released a report dealing with arrests, number of police, and their salaries on a national basis. The report, however, covered the period of 1972 to 1976 only. A summary of the report was published by Canadian Press, and appeared in the *Toronto Globe and Mail*, April 20, 1978, at p. 8.

By year end 1976 there were 51,629 full-time police in Canada, about one for every 450 Canadians. This represents a 10 per cent force increase over 1972. In support of the 51,629 police was a civilian staff of 12,046.

The largest force in the country was the RCMP with 18,662 on the rolls, 14,012 of them police. The Ontario Provincial Police had 5,233 on the rolls, 4,064 of them police, and the Quebec Police 5,170, 4,194 of them police. Among the cities Metropolitan Toronto had the biggest municipal force with a total of 6,605, including 5,534 police. Montreal was next with 5,138 police, followed by Winnipeg, 993, Vancouver, 915, Calgary, 869, Edmonton, 843, Hamilton-Wentworth, 678, Ottawa, 571, Niagara, 527, Peel Region, 525, and Waterloo Region, 426.

The police bill to the nation as a whole in 1976 was about $1 billion a year. The RCMP alone cost $500 million to run in 1976-77. More than $380 million of this was for salaries. First-constables, force members for about five years, then earned $20,000 annually.

The Face of Crime

These are the words of an ex-inmate of the Canadian prison system:

Contrary to what you see on television, the average con is not a master criminal but one of life's losers, with little formal education or skills. He usually has some form of drug problem and a high proportion of them have physical defects such as rotten teeth or misshapen features and although they pretend to the contrary, the majority of them have a very low opinion of themselves. Basically, they are people who cannot function in our competitive, complex society.

From "Like It Is," cited by John Braithwaite in "Refuge of Failure" in *The Criminal Justice System in Canada*, (Jayewardene, C.H.S., ed., University of Ottawa, 1975).

See also, *Waiting for the Ice-Cream Man: A Prison Journal — Manitoba 1978* (Krotz, Larry, ed., Winnipeg: Converse Press, 1978), p. 51:

In Manitoba prisons, half of the inmates are native Indian or Metis though that group of people make up only ten per cent of the province's population. In 1977, 37% of the inmates at Stony Mountain Institution were Native as were 56% of the inmates at Headingley Correctional Institution, 80% at the Portage Centre for Women, and 90% at the jail in The Pas.

The inmate who shows us through the Headingley jail is a striking, dark, handsome young man from Norway House, a village at the top of Lake Winnipeg. He says, though, that he hasn't been back there since 1965. Two of his brothers are also at Headingley.

Jail, sadly, in the experience of Native males is something equivalent to university in the experience of the white middle class. It is something you expect to be a part of your experience as you reach adulthood. Eddie, 27, sits at Headingley through the winter and into the long days of spring making leather belts from a kit. If an uncle, father, cousins, brothers have been there before, it becomes part of your expectation too. Eddie has been to Headingley twice before. This time he is there because he insists on driving even though his licence has been suspended for life.

A Winnipeg Native courtworker says that the institutionalizing of Native people began at the same place that the break-down of their family and community structure did; with the wholesale packing off of Native children to residential schools. "After living in a residential school for fifteen years," she says, "if I committed a crime it would be easy for me to go to Kingston or Portage and do the time because I grew up in an Institution."

The story of Emanuel Jaques was taken from a combination of newspaper reports and confidential interviews with Metropolitan Toronto police and civic officials. For a sampling of the newspaper coverage see, the *Globe and Mail*, August 9, 1977, p. 1; the *Sunday Star*, March 12, 1978, p. A4; the *New York Times*, March 26, 1978, p. 9.

Interviews confirmed the "political" effect of the murder. It was the belief of some in government that before the murder the city was seen as acting too quickly, "moving too fast" to clean up the Strip. After the murder the city was seen as acting too slowly. The point is, however, that the city was given the political "green light" to proceed with its clean-up effort.

There is a point in asking just what the Strip clean-up was to accomplish. To some it meant eliminating the more obvious forms of street solicitation, "body rub" prostitution, and the sale of obscene materials. To others it meant a "total" clean-up, that is, eliminating the Strip. The Law Reform Commission of Canada published a working paper, "Limits of Criminal Law — Obscenity: A Test Case," (Information Canada, 1975). At p. 45 it was stated:

Lastly, one final snag. Use criminal law against obscenity and perhaps we obscure the real problem. To take an analogy, our criminal law has concerned itself with non-medical use of drugs, but may not the real problem be the overall use of drugs in the modern "chemical" society? So with obscenity. The law concerns itself with "undue exploitation of sex," but may not the real problem be something else — our society's reluctance to be open and direct in dealing with sexual matters? Sex is a basic human drive but also something calling for maturity.

Obscenity, however, is immaturity. Obscenity is at odds with personal growth. At best, as in a dirty joke or filthy postcard, it is, as Orwell pointed out, a sort of mental rebellion against a conspiracy to pretend that human nature has no baser side. At worst, it is, as D. H. Lawrence said, an attempt "to insult sex, to do dirt on sex." Neither obscenity nor the law relating to it helps towards a maturer view of sex.

A Morality Play? — The Criminal Trial

The role of the criminal trial as a morality play was stressed by the Law Reform Commission in *Our Criminal Law* (Information Canada, 1976):

> If criminal law has to do with affirming fundamental values, the criminal trial is *par excellence* the place where this is done. The trial is not just directed at the offender in the dock nor even at potential offenders outside. On the contrary, it is a public demonstration to denounce the crime and re-affirm the values it infringed. It is, as Morton aptly showed, a sort of morality play for all of us. The trial is a kind of public theatre in the round.
>
> As such, the solemn trial is appropriate only for real crimes. Whether X robbed Y or murdered Z is a paradigm case of something fit for this species of morality play. Whether A's weights were out of line or B's food incorrectly labelled needs careful public investigation but is clearly not the stuff for solemn public ritual. The full treatment, then, should be reserved for real crimes. [p. 23].

A Crown prosecutor has written: "If the adversary system is to work, the two combatants must be kept equal or at least relatively equal. If one is much stronger than the other, the superior side will gain a substantial advantage and thus undermine a proper determination. For in that event, true conflict is minimized and the outcome is determined simply by superior power. Hence, the proper functioning of the defence is as vital to the adversary system as the prosecuting and judicial functions. If the accused faces the state's prosecuting structure without benefit of advice or assistance of counsel, or such advice or assistance is delayed, the right to challenge the prosecution, which is indispensable to the operation of the adversary system, is gravely impaired."

The trial for murder became something other than probing for the answer to a simple question. There were defenses and technical rules that defense counsel were duty bound to invoke for their clients. In no small way they were assisted by the Crown attorney. The Crown attorney is not a carbon copy of the television version of the American prosecutor. "The position of the Crown attorney is not that of ordinary counsel in a civil case; he is acting in a quasi-judicial capacity or as a minister of justice and ought regard himself as part of the court rather than as an advocate. He is not to struggle for a conviction nor be betrayed by feelings of professional rivalry to regard the question and issue as one of professional superiority and a contest of skill and preeminence." These are the words of a senior Crown attorney.

The Crown attorney was only a kind of adversary in the trial of those charged with the murder of Emanuel Jaques. His office was to be used to ensure that the rule of law was followed. He was no person's protagonist. (See Grosman, Brian A., *The Prosecutor: An Inquiry into the Exercise of Discretion* (University of Toronto Press, 1969) pp. 84-86.)

The standard for determining sanity is firmly embedded in the criminal law, even though less is required in the civil courts to relieve one of responsibility. For example, where property rights are involved, both medical and lay opinions are carefully weighed in finding responsibility. Medical psychotics cannot make enforceable contracts. Or, if unsoundness of mind is properly urged, executed wills will not be probated. Similarly, an "irrational" person might be held incapable of managing affairs, and a guardian would be appointed to take charge of both the person and his property. All of the civil standards listed require far less than the criminal law for a finding of incapacity. Why then does the difference exist? Why shouldn't the criminal law with its penalties require more rather than less for responsibility to attach? The answer may be that given by an English judge who said: "Insanity, from a medical point of view, is one thing; insanity from the point of view of the criminal law is a different thing. Doctors exist to cure physical and mental ills. Judges and juries exist to guard the life and property and the welfare of society."

For a general statement see, the working paper, "The Criminal Process and Mental Disorder" (the Law Reform Commission of Canada, Information Canada, 1975), p. 5. On any day in 1974 there were about 60,000 Canadians in psychiatric institutions, nearly three times the number in prisons.

It is possible for an accused to be held for quite lengthy periods without ever coming to trial. The working paper discusses this possibility on p. 37:

> The accused was charged with theft. He pleaded not guilty and was prepared through counsel to meet the charge with a defence of alibi. But because he was congenitally retarded he was found unfit and his trial postponed. Assuming his defence was valid, being found unfit placed him in an untenable position. If he could proceed to trial he would be acquitted, but he couldn't be tried because he was unfit. So he was detained in a mental hospital until he became fit. But he would never be fit. He would never be returned to trial and therefore never be acquitted. The net effect was to condemn without trial a person not convicted of a crime to a lifetime of psychiatric detention — all in the name of fairness to him. The injustice is obvious and must be avoided. Present procedures, however, afford only limited protection.

Bargain Basement Justice

For crime statistics relating to Ontario see *Criminal Justice Statistics in Ontario* (Ontario Secretariat for Justice, 1977). See also "Restitution and Compensation," in *Community Participation in Sentencing* (Law Reform Commission of Canada, 1976), p. 21.

The statistics relating to those held in penal institutions were cited in the working paper, "Imprisonment and Release" (Law Reform Commission of Canada, 1975), at p. 6. The working paper continued:

DISCOUNT JUSTICE

A study by the Commission showed that one out of every seven persons appearing in court for the first time in Canada and convicted of a non-violent offence against property was imprisoned. On a second conviction for a non-violent property offence almost 50 per cent of offenders were imprisoned. In the light of this type of information we must ask, what do we hope to accomplish by using imprisonment? Far from having fulfilled its humanitarian expectations, imprisonment today is seen to be a costly sanction that ought only to be used as a last resort. It is costly to society, to the prisoners and to the guards and prison officials as individuals. How do these costs manifest themselves? To keep a person in a prison costs around $14,000 a year depending upon the nature of the institution. In addition there are the indirect costs arising out of welfare and increased social services to the prisoner's family. It is difficult to see how an expenditure of $14,000 can be justified unless the harm done is correspondingly high and cannot be paid back except through imprisonment.

The statement concerning alcohol-related offences was quoted in the *Globe and Mail*, June 28, 1978, on p. 1. The details of the British Columbia heroin user programme were set out in the *New York Times*, May 1, 1978, at p. A19. Again, the Law Reform Commission report, *Our Criminal Law*, referred to above, emphasizes the role of the community. (See page 6 of that report.)

NOTES
Chapter Two

An Assembly Line without Direction

See, Wilson, James Q., *Thinking About Crime*, (New York: Basic Books, 1975). The study concerning recent crime in Canada and public fear was reported popularly in the *Toronto Star*, October 23, 1976, p. 1. John Hogarth, a leading Canadian criminologist, said, "The problem of violent crime and juvenile delinquency on the streets is more important in the public mind than economic issues."

While Hogarth might have exaggerated somewhat his reasoning is nonetheless perceptive: Canadians are influenced by crime in the United States in shaping their own views. Yet, the fact is that the U.S. rate for violent crime was 458.8 per 100,000 inhabitants, compared with 98.6 for Canada in 1974. For a factual comment on the American scene see, the *New York Times*, January 15, 1978, at p. 34: "The mood of a three-day hearing in Manhattan on violence was set by a participating criminologist who told the House of Representatives subcommittee [on violent crime] that, according to a recent survey, 'about half the American people will be afraid to walk home alone tonight for fear that they will not make it alive.'" See also, *Time*, "The Youth Crime Plague," July 11, 1977, p. 12.

Fear of violence is real. The following story was reported in the *Toronto Star*, October 27, 1976, p. B1:

> The Osters have had it with the big city. The family of seven is moving back to the Keswick area and what clinched their decision was an incident in which the eldest daughters were threatened. Kim Oster, 20 and Jamie, 18, had just walked out of the bus depot after arriving at 11 p.m. from Keswick. They were immediately followed by two young men. "I said, 'buzz-off, leave us alone.'" Kim said. "They became very upset. They cursed us and hit the wall with their fists. One of them said he wanted to rape me."
> At that time, a man the girls described as in his 60s carrying a black bag, went up to the two youths at Dundas St. W. and Bay St. and said: "Would you please leave those girls alone?" The man was punched, knocked to the ground and his glasses broken, the girls said. Police caught two youths, aged 19 and 20, and charged them with assault, but by the time they had arrived the "old man," as the girls described him, had gone. "We want to find him to pay for his glasses," Jamie said. "The thing that upset us," Kim said, "was that there were big strong men standing around while all this was happening. I don't know what is the matter with people."

DISCOUNT JUSTICE

The details concerning the changing age profile of the Canadian population can be found in *Study on Population and Technology, Perceptions 2*, (Science Council of Canada, Ottawa, 1976) and *Perspective Canada* (Ottawa, 1974).

The comments of Mr. Maloney are found in *The Criminal Justice System in Canada* (Jaywardene, C.H.S. ed., University of Ottawa, 1975), at pp. 148, 153, 158.

As previously indicated, the national statistics relating to crime are difficult to obtain. Some tabular data come from the 1974 publication of Statistics Canada, *Perspective Canada*, at pp. 292, 294:

ADULTS CHARGED, BY OFFENCE GROUP

	1962	1964	1966	1968	1970
		per cent			
Criminal Code	33.4	33.6	30.5	33.8	38.7
Federal Statutes	6.3	5.3	5.6	6.1	6.4
Provincial Statutes	49.3	53.1	54.7	50.0	46.3
Municipal By-laws	11.0	8.0	9.2	10.1	8.6
TOTALS	100.0	100.0	100.0	100.0	100.0
Thousands charged	369	409	468	491	509

JUVENILES CHARGED, BY OFFENCE GROUP

	1962	1964	1966	1968	1970
		per cent			
Criminal Code	82.4	80.5	75.0	79.0	82.9
Federal Statutes	2.6	3.4	2.4	3.1	3.4
Provincial Statutes	10.8	13.7	17.2	13.8	11.4
Municipal By-laws	4.2	2.4	5.4	4.1	2.3
TOTALS	100.0	100.0	100.0	100.0	100.0
Number of juveniles	31,913	45,464	52,956	66,327	63,140

OFFENCE RATE BY PROVINCE[1]

	1962	1964	1966	1968	1970
CANADA	5,165	5,986	6,517	7,508	8,459
Newfoundland	3,354	4,308	4,882	5,778	6,296
Prince Edward Island	4,445	5,556	6,858	7,543	8,001
Nova Scotia	4,738	5,876	6,149	6,704	7,520
New Brunswick	2,884	4,362	5,517	5,808	6,054
Quebec	3,310	3,674	4,069	4,880	5,329
Ontario	5,285	6,233	6,617	7,679	8,882

Manitoba	5,725	6,424	6,625	8,172	9,372
Saskatchewan	6,592	6,775	7,579	8,961	10,050
Alberta	7,596	8,599	9,483	10,704	12,471
British Columbia	8,760	10,389	11,232	12,067	12,732
Yukon[2]	. . .	. . .	. . .	28,675	33,331
Northwest Territories[2]	. . .	. . .	. . .	22,803	31,929

1) *Rate per 100,000 of population seven years and older.*
2) *Because of small population base, Yukon and Northwest Territories rates not calculated before 1967.*

More current data is derived from Canada's largest metropolitan police force, namely, that of Metropolitan Toronto. See, *Metropolitan Toronto Police — Annual Report 1977*, p. 25. This sets out not only offences but their relationship to police resources:

CRIMINAL CODE OFFENCES

	1976	1977
Murder	50	55
Attempt Murder	30	48
Manslaughter	2	0
Rape	189	263
Wounding	404	431
Assaults (Not indecent)	9,342	9,987
Robbery	1,840	1,783
Break and Enter	17,608	18,661
Theft Over (Not Motor Vehicle)	10,531	12,310
Motor Vehicle Thefts	6,356	5,989
Total Index Crime	46,352	49,527
Total Non-Index Crime	148,719	150,190
TOTAL	195,071	199,717

RELATED GROWTH STATISTICS

	1976	1977
Population	2,189,865	2,226,188*
Police Personnel	6,605	6,734
Criminal Code Occ.	195,071	199,717
Crime Rate Per 1,000 population	89.1	89.9
C.C. Offences Cleared	108,643	111,838
% C.C. Offences Cleared	55.7	56.0
Motor Vehicle Reg.	977,422	1,014,122*
Persons Charged	91,983	100,285
Summonses Served	444,560	518,251
Warrants Executed	97,604	115,910
Kilometres by Police Vehicles	38,796,593	39,945,811

*Estimate

DISCOUNT JUSTICE

OTHER OFFENCES

	1976	1977
Federal Statutes	6,972	8,794
Highway Traffic Act	610,405	597,010
Liquor License Act	24,324	29,067
Other Provincial Statutes	2,276	2,384
TOTAL	643,977	637,255

For a discussion of plea bargaining see, Grosman, Brian A., *The Prosecutor: An Inquiry into the Exercise of Discretion* (University of Toronto Press, 1969), pp. 41-47. See also, *Guidelines — Dispositions and Sentences in the Criminal Process*, Law Reform Commission of Canada (Information Canada, 1976), pp. 15-16:

5. The Prosecution: Pre-trial Settlement

5.1. Crown prosecutors should exercise discretion in the selection of cases for pre-trial settlement or prosecution in accordance with express policies and criteria.

5.2. Such policies should be developed by the appropriate ministers in consultation with citizens broadly representative of the community and be complementary to screening policies and criteria developed by police.

5.3. Policy directives should encourage the screening out of cases from the criminal process, where feasible and identify situations similar to those under 4.5.

5.4. Criteria should be developed in conjunction with a policy to screen cases out of the criminal justice system similar to those under 4.6.

5.5. Where a charge is laid, the crown prosecutor may refer the case to a community agency or resource person for pre-trial settlement and advise the Justice before whom the information was sworn accordingly.

5.6. Once a case has reached the stage of court appearance, disposition other than a termination of the prosecution should require judicial approval.

5.7. Pre-trial settlements should be made in accordance with express criteria which may include the following:
   (a) the circumstances of the event are not serious enough to warrant prosecution, although the evidence would support a prosecution;
   (b) the circumstances show a prior relationship between the victim and the offender;
   (c) the facts of the case are not substantially in dispute;
   (d) the offender and victim voluntarily accept the offered pre-trial settlement as an alternative to prosecution and trial;
   (e) the needs and interests of society, the offender and the victim can be better served through a pre-trial settlement than through conviction and sentence;
   (f) trial and conviction may cause undue harm to the victim or offender or otherwise result in unreasonable social costs.

5.8. No sanction may be imposed upon an offender without his consent in non-judicial methods of disposition.

5.9. Records of pre-trial settlements should be kept to ensure visibility and accountability.

Ontario's Attorney General accepted only a portion of the proposed guidelines. The authors of the guidelines, he said, operated in a "rarified atmosphere . . . somewhat detached from the real world." The Attorney General would only have required that the results of plea bargaining be made a part of the court record. See the *Toronto Star*, Feb. 24, 1976, p. 1.

The Victim: Left in the Cold

The case of Harold Hilton is set out in "Unhappy Owners Lose Out. . . .," *Globe and Mail*, July 3, 1978, at p. 18. See also, Zegenhagin, Edward M., *Victims, Crime and Social Control* (New York: Praeger, 1977):

> Benefits can arise from use of restitution by offenders to victims. The first is that it repairs the relationship between victim and offender. The second is that it gives a specific understandable goal to the offender, unlike the vague "rehabilitation." Third, restitution demands the participation of the offender in some constructive enterprise. This requirement again is in contrast to the passivity of offenders that can exist in either therapeutic or punitive approaches to rehabilitation. The impact on the offender of restitution is also believed to contribute to development of self-esteem and establishment of self-perception as a responsible member of society. The fourth objective is closely related to the third. . . . the offender may be able to resolve any guilt that has arisen from his participation in a crime. The fifth objective is related to changes in the community's perception of the offender. In this instance, restitution is believed to entail a more positive response from the community toward the offender who is attempting to contribute to redress of the wrongs suffered by the victim.

The development of the criminal law in terms of keeping fines for the state rather than the victim are discussed in working papers, "Restitution and Compensation," in *Community Participation in Sentencing* (Law Reform Commission of Canada, 1976), pp. 8-9. See also, "Fines," in the same work, p. 32.

Crime and Profit to the State

Professor Linden's comments are contained in, "Restitution, Compensation for Victims of Crime and Canadian Criminal Law," *Community Participation in Sentencing* (Law Reform Commission of Canada, 1976), pp. 7, 35. In his paper Professor Linden added:

> Restitution plays a minor role in Canadian criminal justice today. Primarily, it is used in theft, fraud and malicious damage cases, where the accused appears able to repay the owner of the property he has taken or damaged. The full potential of restitution has never been achieved nor even seriously studied. Corrections officials have almost nothing to do with the problem, because virtually no one presently in prison is under any obligation to make restitution. Many of these prison authorities support the idea of restitution but they have no control at all over the sentencing function of the courts. Judges, with rare exceptions, do not concern themselves very much with restitution. Crown counsel seldom seek restitution for they have little to do with the victims, who are merely the prosecutors' witnesses. The police rarely make requests for restitution. The victim is seldom aware of his rights. Occasionally, he may ask

the police or the Crown for restitution or he may speak out in court. One Crown counsel told me of an incident where a complainant in an assault charge, during the sentencing, stood up in court waving his broken eyeglasses in the air. He took the hint, asked for restitution for the cost of the glasses and it was ordered by the court as a condition of probation.

The most important instigator of restitution today seems to be the defence counsel. One might expect that the interest of his client would be in conflict with that of the victim. This is wrong. When defence counsel seeks to arrange for restitution he is doing it in his client's interest alone. It is only coincidentally that it serves the victim as well in that he gets the benefit of a restitution order. Nevertheless, it is in the interest of the offender to demonstrate to the court that he has repented and that he wishes to make amends. If he repays the money or property taken or if he pays damages to his victim, his sentence will probably be reduced. [p. 43].

NOTES
Chapter Three

The Victim and the Courts

Too often the victim does stand alone. See Calvin Becker, "Statistical Follow-up of Criminal Occurrences in Toronto Patrol Area 5411: An Examination of the Relationship Between Victims and Offenders," in *Studies on Diversion*, Law Reform Commission of Canada (Ottawa: Information Canada, 1975), p. 175. At pp. 194-198 the story of Mike is told. He operated a corner milk store in a Toronto residential-commercial area. In a period of five years he was robbed five times. What follows is a partial interview:

MIKE: The time I was robbed when the guy just put the thing on my back I was more scared of the bottle of pop 'cause I don't know if they're going to take my money and give it to me over the head — I didn't mind the shot 'cause that would kill me. The thing was, I didn't see what was on my back, but I saw the bottle and I thought they're going to kill you, but they're going to go ahead and hit you on the head with the bottle and you think that's how the thing will be over. . . .

I had about two years and it was quiet, and now in two or three weeks I have the two robberies. The thing is, I'm by myself in the store all the time. That makes it easier, you know, to rob me. They know I'm by myself all day and night so that's easier. Most of the stores, they have two guys.

INTERVIEWER: How is it you never have any help?

MIKE: I don't need it, I guess, I don't need help. I don't need someone to help me, just to protect me. . . .

Well, I'm frightened many times you know, about the job. I couldn't stand it and I'm not sure I'm going to stay. You see, I'm scared for everybody. If somebody comes behind my counter to look for something I get frightened. . . . I get more tired of the three hours at night than for the eleven hours in the morning, more tired from those last three hours, 'cause I'm scared and I try most of the time to keep myself in the back, near the freezer. I don't like to stand behind the counter. . . . I like to leave the door [pointing to the rear door] open a ways sometimes so I could run out. It's funny, you know, it can be — and I'm sick, I'm upset after someone would rob me. . . . It makes me nervous. You see, I was happy in my job, you know. I liked it to work in my store, I like to talk to the customers. . . . Sometimes people, you know them, you don't want to be scared but still you are scared. Sometimes I am thinking to myself, there's nobody in the store now. Sometimes at night, I think who's going to come in now, you know, who's going to get in, you open the door and you know him. . . .

> Like I was saying now, if you get a guy who is shoplifting, you call the police, they come here, they get the name — and you have the guy and they still want you to go to court, you know, to lose all your day. I think that's the police, they should have the guy right away in court. Why don't they do it? . . . They get paid for all this, you know, sending a guy to court. . . . But I see them and they ask me, do you want to go to court with that guy, and I say, no, it doesn't matter, so they let him go. . . . You have nothing about it for fifty cents, to go to court, the police should go — that's how they do it in my country [Greece].

See also McDonald, William F. ed., *Criminal Justice and the Victim* (Beverly Hills, California: Sage Publications, 1976).

Dr. Justin Ciale wrote of the control of bank robbery in Montreal in "Crime Prevention and Control," in *Crime Prevention Through Community Control*, (Vancouver: Centre for Continuing Education, University of British Columbia, 1972), at p. 6. The long term effect of such action is questionable. In 1977 the president of the Canadian Bankers' Association referred to Montreal as "the hold-up capital of the world." For all of Canada during the first nine months of 1977 there was a total of 781 violent crimes against banks. Of this total, 581 occurred in Quebec (mostly in Montreal). In the same period in 1976 a total of 424 violent crimes against banks occurred in Quebec. See, the *Toronto Star*, Nov. 16, 1977, p. C11.

The cases involving fines to assist victims are not numerous. The British Columbia case referred to in the text is: *Regina v. Dashner*, (British Columbia Court of Appeal) *Western Weekly Reports* 11 (1974). McFarlane, J.A., who spoke for the court stated:

> I think assistance in the task of interpretation and application of s. 663(2)(e) [of the Criminal Code] may be found in para. (h) which authorizes:
> ". . . such other reasonable conditions as the court considers desirable for securing the good conduct of the accused and for preventing a repetition by him of the same offence or the commission of other offences."
> It appears that the general purpose of probation orders is to secure the good conduct of the convicted person as opposed to compensating victims of crime. The remedies available to them by ordinary civil suit and under the Criminal Injuries Compensation Act, 1972 (B.C.), c. 17, should not be overlooked: nor the difference between compensation on the one hand and restitution or reparation on the other.
>
> It may be useful to repeat what was said by this Court when dealing with the application of s. 638(2)(b) [repealed 1968-69, c. 38, s. 75] of the Criminal Code, 1953-54, c. 51, in *Regina v. Stewart*, 63 W.W.R. 442 at 445, [1968] 4 C.C.C. 54:
> "It may be observed that the appeal has been disposed of on what might be described as rather technical grounds. It must be remembered, however, that it is most important that the sanctions of the criminal law and its administration should not be used, or be permitted to appear to be used, for the purpose of enforcing civil obligations. For this reason I think it is essential that careful regard should be given to the ability of an accused to pay when a court sees fit to exercise the power, conferred by sec. 638(2)(a), to prescribe as a condition of release that there be restitution and reparation to an aggrieved or injured person. The same considerations apply when it is proposed to change the conditions prescribed for such a purpose. The responsibility for prescribing the conditions is that of the court which has therefore the duty to form a judicial

opinion of the accused's ability to comply. If it were otherwise we might well find that imprisonment for debt has not been truly abolished."

I agree with the argument of counsel for the Crown that no separate or formal inquiry is a necessary preliminary to the prescribing of a condition under s. 663(2)(e). There should, however, in my opinion, be facts before the sentencing judge to show that the amount of restitution or reparation ordered is for actual loss or damage sustained by the person aggrieved or injured and that the convicted person has the means to pay it.

In the present case I think there was insufficient evidence of these matters and the conditions complained of must be expunged from the orders. I think this Court is not in a position to assess different amounts with any reasonable assurance. For example, Mrs. Broadfoot's injuries are described by the trial Judge as "not of an extensive nature," while in the case of Morgan it was said "he received a terrific beating."

Counsel for the Crown submitted that if the conditions be removed the fines should be increased. I am bound to say that having regard to the nature of the assaults and the appellant's criminal record, I think the two fines of $250 each amount to a very lenient sentence. The appellant was not given notice of intention by the Crown to ask for a greater punishment. Having regard to the present practice of the court in that respect and to the paucity of relevant information, I do not feel justified in increasing the amount of the fines.

Professor Linden's study relating to fines and compensation to victims can be found in A. M. Linden, "Compensation For Victims of Crime and Canadian Criminal Law," *Community Participation in Sentencing*, Law Reform Commission of Canada (Ottawa, 1976), p. 3.

The case of Sam and the attempted rape is reported in *Regina v. A.* (Ontario High Court of Justice), *The Criminal Law Quarterly* volume 17, (September 25, 1974), p. 115.

In *Re Torek and The Queen* (Ontario High Court), 15 *Canadian Criminal Cases* (Jan. 8, 1974), p. 296, Mr. Justice Heines stated at pp. 298-299:

Counsel for the applicant argued forcefully that s. 653 is really legislation pertaining to property and civil rights and falls within the ambit of s. 92(13) of the *British North America Act, 1867*, rather than criminal law. Counsel pointed out that under s. 653, the accused is deprived of many of the protections which he would have in an ordinary civil action. For instance, the defendant does not really have notice of the claim beforehand and cannot defend it properly. He has no right to discovery by which he could attempt to elicit proper proof of value of the articles which allegedly have been stolen. In the present case, one of the articles allegedly stolen by the applicant was a ring owned by Mrs. Kaminsky. The value of that ring was placed at $1,500, but no proof of purchase or of the value of the ring was led before the Court. In arriving at the sum of $4,377.50, His Honour Judge Reville clearly accepted Mr. Kaminsky's testimony as to exactly what was stolen in cash, the ring and liquor. The applicant argues that had Mr. Kaminsky been forced to undertake a civil action to recover the sum, he would have been forced to prove his loss in a stricter manner. However, under s. 653, all that the complainant need do is merely testify as to value and the accused cannot really disprove it. In other words, the protection afforded to a defendant by the *Judicature Act*, R.S.O. 1970, c. 228, and the Rules of Practice, are removed, but the consequence is really the same in the sense in that the complainant gets what is, in effect, a judgment, which by s. 653(2) can be enforced in the provincial superior Courts in the ordinary manner.

I do not think that there can be any doubt that the right to bring and defend an ordinary civil action is a civil right, which is within the competence of provincial legislation. Nor can there be any doubt that in these circumstances, Mr. Kaminsky could have commenced an action against the applicant. However, it does not follow that the federal Government is entirely without power to order restitution or compensation in some circumstances.

In my view, proceedings under s. 653 can be considered to be part of the sentencing process. It is worth noting that in s. 601, which deals with appeals on indictable offences, the word "sentence" is defined to include an order made under s. 653. It seems to me that it is a valid object in sentencing to prevent a convicted criminal from profiting from his crime by serving a jail term and then keeping the gains of his illegal venture. Counsel for the applicant admitted that it would be proper for the order complained of to have been made as a term of probation, pursuant to s. 663(2)(e) and (h), which state that the Court may impose as a condition of a probation order, conditions that the accused:

> "(e) make restitution or reparation to any person aggrieved or injured
>   by the commission of the offence for the actual loss or damage
>   sustained by that person as a result thereof;
> "(f) comply with such other reasonable conditions as the court
>   considers desirable for securing the good conduct of the accused
>   and for preventing a repetition by him of the same offence or the
>   commission of other offences."

I fail to see that there is any meaningful distinction between an order requiring an accused to make restitution or reparation as set out in s. 663(2)(e) and an order requiring an accused to pay by way of satisfaction or compensation as set out in s. 653(1).

The Victim and the Criminal Meet

Professor Linden reported the story of the travel agent who preferred prison to restitution, *op. cit., supra*, at pp. 43-44. Professor Schafer is cited and quoted by Professor Linden at pp. 39-40. See, Schafer, Stephen, *Compensation and Restitution to Victims of Crime* (2d ed., 1970).

The all-party report on federal prisons is most important. It sets out the costs of housing an inmate and the reality of work for pay. See, *Report to Parliament*, The Sub-Committee on the Penitentiary System in Canada, Standing Committee on Justice and Legal Affairs, Mark MacGuigan, Chairman, Second Session, 30th Parliament, 1976-77 (1977) at pp. 17, 106, 108:

> 81.   The cost of maintaining an inmate in prison is estimated at $17,515 a year
> for each male, maximum security prisoner. It is cheaper for society to try
> reformation than to nurture recidivists who could spend 25 years or more in
> prison at a cost of $400,000 each. The true gain in social betterment is
> incalculable.
> 505.   A prison that has not solved the problem of prison labour cannot be said
> to be operating an institution of correction and reform. There is little chance of
> reforming an inmate who, upon his release, is unwilling, unable, or unfit to
> accept employment. In most cases, it is only by inspiring the inmate to pursue

creative and productive work habits that any lasting value will be obtained from the expense of imprisoning him.

506. We therefore believe that every inmate who is physically capable of working should be required to work, and the situation in which large numbers spend most, or perhaps all, of their time in enforced idleness should not be permitted. The employment facilities in the institutions should, so far as possible, be designed to meet the individual training needs of inmates and should duplicate the production methods of industry in free society, so that an inmate, upon his release, will have a reasonable hope of being a competitive member of the labour market. There should, moreover, be a meaningful correlation between the amount of work done by an inmate and the pay he receives.

507. In 1914, a Royal Commission on Penitentiaries recommended the establishment of an industrial workshop system in penitentiary institutions in order to meet the material needs of the government. Moreover, the promotion of work programs outside the walls for inmates was strongly supported. It was only in 1950 that a Committee of Ministers was established in order to develop, within government agencies, an adequate market to absorb the products of penitentiary industries. The positive results, brought about by that Committee, raised new problems: by 1970, penitentiary industry was responsible for the carrying out of 2000 small contracts yearly. These related to 760 production lines for 1100 customers, including government agencies and non-profit enterprises, producing brushes, boxes and other items. This gave rise to undue pressure being brought to bear on instructors, in order to control short production lines within workshops overcrowded with inmates, very few of whom were actually working.

517. The truth is, of course, that very few inmates in our federal institutions are actually engaged in prison industry, and those that are, are not particularly well motivated. It is in the interest of both the inmates and the Penitentiary Service to improve the industrial program. But this cannot be done so long as penitentiaries retain their present, outmoded means of production, nor while some inmates are paid as little as seventy-five cents a day for their labour. If the industries are to function with a degree of efficiency at least somewhat akin to that of industry in free society, major changes in our approach to inmate labour must be made.

518. As early as 1970, the Department of the Solicitor General responded to the chronic state of inactivity of the inmates. This situation led in April 1973 to the issuance of the *Report on Prison Industries Re-Orientation* prepared by the Management Consulting Service. Of the seventeen recommendations in this report most were accepted by the C.P.S. The recommendations included:
   —the necessity of simulating conditions similar to the outside economy;
   —the importance of an adequate salary for the inmates, according to their skills, production and experience;
   —the establishment of a remuneration system for over-production, ranging from group bonuses to accelerated deserved remission;
   —a higher wage system for the other types of activities for those working in the industry;
   —the right of the workshop foreman to select his staff (pp. 58-60).

519. This report contains an inmate wage plan which would place inmate wages near the minimum wage, and it stresses the necessity for the inmate to cover the expenses incurred for him by the Government. We support these proposals. Furthermore, Canadian penitentiary industries are compared unfavorably to the U.S. system, where the industries are organized into state enterprises, whose profits are used for the improvement of the already existing education programs.

520. Even though the C.P.S. is now oriented towards the industrialization of its enterprises and its workshops through profitable activities, which would provide an acceptable profitability margin, the establishment of this system is nevertheless very slow. The Sub-Committee underlines the necessity of implementing these recommendations and notes that at present maximum security penitentiaries would benefit most by the early adoption of this approach.

Professor Linden, *op. cit. supra*, discusses criminal injuries compensation. For examples of the direction taken see the annual reports of the *Ontario Criminal Injuries Compensation Board.* See also, D. R. Miers, "The Ontario Criminal Injuries Compensation Scheme," 24 *University of Toronto Law Journal* 347 (1974). As to pain and suffering as elements in a compensation scheme Mr. Miers argued at p. 368:

> With respect, the reasons adduced for denying the victim any compensation for pain and suffering are not altogether convincing. It would seem that despite the victim's state of euphoria, some pain and suffering was experienced at the time of the assault, and this should surely justify an award. However, the main criticism of the board's reasoning in *Blair* is that the reasons adduced are inappropriate to the issue of pain and suffering. Where such an award is denied at common law, it is because the victim did not experience any pain arising out of the incident which caused his injuries, and, while the board is correct in principle, their argument goes to loss of amenities rather than pain suffered at the time of the injury. It has authoritatively been held that incapacity on the part of the victim to appreciate his disability is irrelevant in the assessment of damages for loss of amenities, but this has nothing to do with pain and suffering. In any event the consideration of loss of amenities is not within the board's jurisdiction.

In Aid of the Victim: A Proposal

The narrow British approach to compensating victims of crime is set out in D. R. Miers, "The Ontario Criminal Injuries Compensation Scheme," 24 *University of Toronto Law Journal* 374 (1974), at p. 368. The Ontario experience in the handling of rape claims is derived from an analysis of the Annual Reports of the Ontario Criminal Injuries Compensation Board. The following is a summary of some of those matters:

> **100-808.** The applicant, twenty years of age, was the victim of a multiple rape by a group of persons who belonged to a motorcycle club. All five offenders pleaded guilty to rape; four of the five were sentenced to six years in prison and the fifth was sentenced to three years.
>
> Award: $1,938 (pain and suffering $1,000).
>
> **100-841.** The victim, a thirty-six-year-old widow, was returning to her home when two young men attempted to force her into their car, with the intention of indecently assaulting her. She sustained dental damage plus minor lacerations. The offenders were not apprehended.
>
> Award: $611.78 (pain and suffering $300).

100-960.   The victim, age fifteen, was brutally assaulted and raped by a casual acquaintance who was charged with rape and indecent assault on a female. He was convicted of both offences and sentenced to a total of seven years in penitentiary.
   Award: $2,376 (pain and suffering $2,000).

200-340.   The victim, a fifty-three-year-old woman, was assaulted and raped in her apartment. The offender was convicted of rape and sentenced to six years in penitentiary.
   Award: $2,904.85 (pain and suffering $2,500).

200-521.   The victim, age forty-five, was brutally attacked and raped by a juvenile assailant. Although she sustained only minor physical injuries, the after-effects of this emotionally traumatic incident were considerable. The offender was found guilty of rape as well as other outstanding charges. He was sentenced to Hillcrest Training School for an indefinite period.
   Award: $2,606 (pain and suffering $2,500).

200-539.   The victim, age forty-five, was raped and brutally assaulted with the result that she lost the sight of one eye and sustained permanent brain damage. One of the two offenders was found guilty of wounding and was sentenced to five years in prison; the other was convicted of being an accessory after the fact and was sentenced to two years, six months in prison.
   Award: $6,660 (pain and suffering $5,000).

200-582.   The victim, age twenty-three, was indecently assaulted after having accepted a ride while hitch-hiking. She sustained minor injuries after having jumped from the vehicle while it was in motion. The offender was convicted of indecent assault and was fined $300 or six months' imprisonment.
   Award: $927.67 (pain and suffering $750).

200-607.   The applicant, age sixty, was the victim of an attempted rape. She was viciously assaulted and sustained facial injuries which required corrective surgery. The offender has not been identified.
   Award: $2,904.25 (pain and suffering $2,500).

   See, "The First Report of the Law Enforcement Compensation Board under the Law Enforcement Compensation Act," 1967 (for the period April 1, 1968 to March 31, 1970) (Ontario) at p. 18. There the board addressed itself to the possibility of financial recovery from the offender:

> The offender is notified where possible. To date, one offender appeared but did not remain for the hearing.
>
> Under Section 7(1), the Board is subrogated to all the rights of the person in whose favour the order is granted in respect to the injury or death to the extent of the amount awarded. We have not made any attempt to keep track of the offenders. Many of them are in jail and the whereabouts of a good number are unknown. We do not consider it would be economically feasible to pursue them. The Chairman of the New York Board told the undersigned Chairman that his Board has never collected from an offender. We have had several cases where the victim had instituted civil proceedings against the offender but was unwilling to continue with those proceedings unless we were willing to underwrite them. In each case, after investigation, we reached the conclusion it was not worth the gamble. Undoubtedly, sooner or later, we will learn at the hearing that the offender has assets, in which case we will take action to recover. But as a matter of policy, the cost of ascertaining the whereabouts of financial resources of offenders generally is prohibitive.

NOTES
Chapter Four

Street Corner Justice

Much of the quoted police comment is taken from Anne Scace, "Criminal Justice and Social Justice: Management of Conflict and Social Disorder by the Metropolitan Toronto Police," in *Studies on Diversion — East York Community Law Reform Project*, Law Reform Commission of Canada (Information Canada, 1975) at pp. 97-124. See page 101:

> The twenty-four-hour visibility of the police, their historical tradition of "helper" and their role of authority make them the public's number one troubleshooters.
> "I had a woman call the station to have an officer come to speak forcefully to her thirty-four-year-old son, to make him go down to the Clarke Institute for his aftercare appointment. . . . He hadn't been taking his medication and he was getting funny again and she was getting scared. . . ."
> However, because the police are not equipped as a health or social service agency, the community's non-criminal problems can and do end up in a criminal justice system that is unable and unsuited to resolve those problems. The marital dispute or domestic quarrel, where there may have been an assault by one of the partners against the other, often results from deeper problems within the family relationship. Is it to be resolved in our present system of justice? Although an offence under the criminal code may have been committed by the husband or wife, is any purpose served by taking the dispute through the adversary system of the courts? The problem that faces the policeman is to decide the best resolution for the situation at hand.
> "You know damn well that most of these crisis things have been going on for years. Then they erupt and the best we can do is hope to cool it down and hope that they can get some help to stop it happening again. But we can be pretty sure that they'll be back in the same boat again and we will have to go back and referee and call the fight. . . ."
> There are three courses of action open to the policeman when he has investigated a reported situation: he can take formal action, that is, he can invoke the criminal process by charging an offender; he can take informal action, by referral to a social agency without charge, or use a charge (later to be dropped) to force a referral; or he can resolve the situation at the time without taking any external action, involving no follow-up by himself o: social agencies. He may not even fill out an "occurrence form" which would be the only record of the incident.
> The action a policeman takes depends not only upon the statutory rules, or the policies and procedures of the Force, but also upon many community

factors that affect the ultimate decision. In many calls to which a policeman responds, a charge under the criminal code could be laid; however, the policeman will often decide that the incident is a social misdemeanour that should not be resolved in the courts. Therefore, in order to understand the role of the police in dealing with "crime," it is essential to come to grips with the meaning of his discretionary power.

See also, Grosman, Brian A., *The Prosecutor: An Inquiry into the Exercise of Discretion* (University of Toronto Press, 1969) pp. 23-27, 43-47.

The Metropolitan Toronto Police report concerning rape victims has been kept confidential for more than three years. It deserves to be mentioned and some of its findings made public. See, *Report of the Police Committee on Rape*, July 30, 1975 (unpublished). This is what the victims said of the police, at pp. 11-12:

The Police
Their general opinion was that the police investigation was satisfactory. Some praised the police, some had minor complaints, and one complained bitterly. The survey team have noted the concerns which women related in the hope that in future investigations of this all victims will have praise for the police. These concerns are as follows:

1. Some found that the uniformed officers who arrived in the first instance gave the impression of being detached and disinterested.
2. Most found plainclothes officers to be more experienced, sympathetic and understanding than uniformed officers.
3. The majority remarked about the number of police officers involved in their cases — initially, during questioning, and during subsequent investigation.
4. Many commented that they were not kept informed of the status of the case, including final disposition.
5. Most were embarrassed to discuss the intimacies of the act with investigators and some of these felt that the male officers were embarrassed as well.
6. The majority expressed the opinion that they would have preferred relating to a mature, experienced female officer. They said that if a woman was not available, they would prefer to speak to an older, mature male (NOT a young policeman or policewoman).
7. Most expressed a desire to have a relative or friend present during the interview. Many who made such requests were refused.
8. Many wondered if the same investigators could not be in charge of the whole case, so that they could relate the facts only once.
9. Many women would prefer that police inform them and explain the reasons for looking into their past, particularly if they intended to interview former boy friends, neighbours, family, etc.
10. Most would appreciate more privacy at police stations. They were of the opinion that everyone wanted to see or talk to them. They would remind police officers that they are not victims by choice.
11. The court procedure was not always explained to witnesses.

Recommendation: That all officers display sincere and continuous concern for the welfare of the rape victim.
Recommendation: That confusion for the rape victim be eliminated by the assignment of a team of mature, experienced investigators, including a woman,

if possible, and that senior supervisors ensure that this team takes charge and remains in charge of the case.

Recommendation: That Staff Sergeants in charge of stations ensure that rape victims have privacy in police buildings.

See also, Goldstein, Herman, *Policing a Free Society*, (Cambridge, Mass.: Bollinger Publishing Company, 1977); Freedman, David J. and Stennig, Philip C., *Private Security, Police, and the Law in Canada*, (Toronto: University of Toronto Press, 1977).

A Person for All Seasons: Job Definition

In addition to the article by Ms. Scace, "Criminal Justice and Social Justice: Management of Conflict and Social Disorder by the Metropolitan Toronto Police," *op. cit. supra*, see, Dunlop, Sheila and Greenway, Denise, *An Examination of the Metropolitan Toronto Police Community Service Officer Programme from Two Viewpoints; The Police and the Community*, (Toronto, 1972); Goldstein, Herman, *Policing a Free Society*, (Cambridge, Mass.: Bollinger Publishing Company, 1977); Muir, William Ker Jr., *Police: Street-corner Politicians*, (Chicago: University of Chicago Press, 1977).

Ms. Scace, *op. cit. supra*, at p. 99 wrote:

> In this age of the specialist, every problem — legal, social or medical — has its special "fixer" and members of the public delegate more and more of their individual responsibilities to the specialists. Unfortunately, the specialists and their institutions frequently are unable to resolve the complex problems that are referred to them. As a consequence, the policeman may be called in to fill the gaps caused by the breakdown of social service agencies in handling crisis situations. Because of his visibility, twenty-four-hour service and role as "protector" the policeman is used as the "specialist" for many non-criminal problems. It is interesting to note that in interviews with citizens concerning their problems and their involvement with the police, many people see their problems as legal or pertaining to the law. It is hard to determine if they originally considered their problems of a legal nature prior to the call to the police or if police intervention denoted the problem as legal, after the fact.
>
> If we are to understand the nature of crime and the function of police in modern society, therefore, it is imperative to the process of law reform or justice planning that the experience and views of the policeman be considered. Because of the unique position of the policeman at the meeting of law and people in trouble, it is increasingly evident that policemen have a valuable contribution to make to the reform of the criminal law.

The Quebec experience concerning police diversion to mental health institutions is set out in the working paper, *The Criminal Process and Mental Disorders*, Law Reform Commission of Canada (Ottawa, 1976) at pp. 25-26.

Statistics relating to the size and cost of the Metropolitan Toronto Police can be found in *Metropolitan Police — Annual Report 1977* (Toronto, 1978). However, it must be emphasized that citizen complaints do occur. Moreover, while the Toronto police generally are held in good repute, very real problems concerning citizen-police relations have arisen in other departments. In

November, 1978, the Ontario Police Commission recommended that Waterloo Regional Chief Sydney Brown, a former member of the Metropolitan Police force and president for many years of its policeman's association, be fired, along with two of the officers under his command, and that two other policemen be reduced in rank. The recommendations came after twenty-nine days of public hearing as a result of two police raids on the Henchmen Motorcycle Club. Twenty persons were taken to regional police headquarters, beaten, bitten by a dog, had knives held at their throats, but were not charged. The Ontario Police Commission stated: "There are stains and blemishes on police history which will be difficult to erase caused by the actions of the above named officers, and others who cannot be identified, but were involved with them in the incidents which resulted in the inquiry." The *Globe and Mail*, November 30, 1978, p. 1.

At times, police illegality can become institutionalized. This seems to be the case with the RCMP in the area of so-called national security. The McDonald Royal Commission has had evidence of systematic RCMP illegal break-ins. See, the *Globe and Mail*, April 20, 1978, p. 1. Editorially the *Globe and Mail* had strong words, April 20, 1978, p. 6:

> The issue arises because of the astounding testimony given to the federal Royal Commission inquiry into the RCMP by Assistant Commissioner Thomas Venner, head of RCMP criminal investigations. Last week Mr. Venner testified that between 1963 and 1974 when wiretap legislation came into force, there were 3,288 wiretaps installed, about 1,000 of which involved entries, including break-ins. Mr. Venner said the RCMP had been told by its legal advisers that because there was no law against wiretaps at that time it was legal to install them and that break-ins for that purpose would be legal. This was because the break and enter section of the Criminal Code prohibits break-ins only where there is an intent to do something illegal once you get inside, Mr. Venner said.
>
> This week, still testifying before the Royal Commission, Mr. Venner said that since 1970, RCMP officers had conducted 419 searches without a search warrant. He called them "surreptitious entry intelligence probes." They were conducted when police did not have enough evidence to obtain a search warrant but where they thought the search would be in the public interest by helping detect crime. At the very least they were "defensible morally and ethically," he said. Again, Mr. Venner said officers had not broken the law in entering without permission because their purpose was not illegal: there is nothing in the Criminal Code which specifically prohibits searches without a warrant.
>
> Once a police officer starts acting according to what he thinks ought to be his role and steps outside the confines of enforcing what the law says, he enters into a perilous realm that can lead him to the most absurd rationalizations. For instance Mr. Venner, having announced the RCMP's right to decree what is in the public interest, comes to believe that RCMP judgment on searches is better than that of a court. It is not always easy to persuade a judge to issue a search warrant, he says. So, rather than "camouflage" the information given to a judge sometimes it is better (because of what the RCMP considers the greater public interest in detecting crime) to conduct a search without a warrant.
>
> Look at what he is saying. Because the RCMP puts itself in the position of substituting its decision for a judge's it finds itself deciding between two

villainous propositions: either mislead or lie to a judge; or violate one of the most fundamental of all legal principles — that a man's home is his castle and will not be invaded without proper authority. That the RCMP is prepared to do either or both, and on the massive kind of scale that Mr. Venner is talking about, surely provides a classic illustration of a police force out of control.

The responsibility for this situation rests, as it must, with the Solicitor-General of Canada. No longer can it be claimed that none of the holders of that office knew what was going on. There were so many break-ins over such a long time they must have known. And if they didn't their ignorance of what was going on was itself so massive that they must bear the responsibility for their own incompetence.

It is time for the Prime Minister to demand some resignations. And time for provincial Attorneys-General to begin investigations preparatory to laying charges at the top.

Working with the Community: Crime Prevention

The remarks of Inspector Heywood can be found in Heywood, R. M., *Community Policing*, Centre for Continuing Education, University of British Columbia (Vancouver, 1972). See also, Scace, *op. cit. supra*, pp. 117-121, where the Toronto police community service officer programme is described. At pp. 120-121 Ms. Scace states:

Domestic disputes have long been the frustrating social problem that police recognize as having a potential for violence and crime; at the same time the police know that the courts in these cases are not equipped to offer satisfactory solutions. The Metro force has undertaken an experiment in one division in an attempt to divert family disputes from the criminal justice system through referral to a community agency for resolution. When a uniformed officer is called to a family dispute he responds to the crisis demands of the situation. However, he makes note of information pertaining to the situation and passes this on to the Community Service Officer as soon as possible. The CSO calls back to speak to the participants in the dispute. He spends as much time as needed to satisfactorily refer the participants to a co-operating family agency which will continue to work with the problem. The results of this project have shown the need to initiate this procedure in other divisions. "If they are able to talk over some of the problems with a social worker who can help them maybe we can prevent another occurrence."

When the public becomes aware of the CSO program, they ask why the entire force cannot be made up of men such as these. This is an impractical demand, for it is essential to have a balance between this type of officer and the calculating, hard-driving, investigative men in Morality, Intelligence, or Homicide. Why? As one police officer stated: "Whether the public knows it or not there are still organized crime and violent criminals in the city and it is essential to have the right type of men dealing with the various elements in our society."

Behaviour of a CSO when promoted, transferred back to the uniformed ranks, and placed in charge of other men is different to that of the man who has not been in the unit and has not had the opportunity for indepth exposure to community problems. Although there have been only a handful of promotions since the unit's inception it is interesting to note that the new CSO-type sergeant encourages his men to be more aware of the community they work in. His technique in arresting will be authoritative but humane, his tolerance for the station paperwork is high; the new sergeant tends to approach situations with a sense of humorous manipulation, rather than hard-line rhetoric. He tends to have an open, assured and interested manner in dealing with public complaints instead of the bored matter-of-factness that can be found in a sergeant who has been on the job longer or in uniform during his whole career. The CSO as a sergeant seems to take an interest in making his constables aware of the variety of ways of using discretion and the available resources. It must be stated, however, that Community Service Officers do not lose their ability to react in strict law enforcement or investigation of criminal offences. As with all police officers, they uphold and rely on the legal statutes and militaristic structure to keep order and protect the public. It is only in the method or use of their discretion that they differ from their uniformed counterparts.

A popular statement of citizen attitude toward the police was commissioned and printed by the *Sunday Star*, August 26, 1978, on p. 3. See also, Goldstein, Herman, *Policing a Free Society*, (Cambridge, Mass., Bollinger Publishing Company, 1977). In April, 1978, Statistics Canada released a report dealing with arrests, number of police, and their salaries on a national basis. See also the *Globe and Mail*, April 20, 1978, p. 8.

The editorial on hanging was printed by the *Sunday Star*, July 16, 1978, at p. A8.

NOTES
Chapter Five

Prisoner Profile

For a general profile of inmates in Canadian prisons see the working paper, "Imprisonment and Release," Law Reform Commission of Canada (Information Canada, 1975) at pp. 5-8. A more detailed source and one rather heavily relied upon in the writing of this chapter is: *Report to Parliament*, the Subcommittee on the Penitentiary System in Canada, Standing Committee on Justice and Legal Affairs, 2d Session, 30th Parliament 1976-77 (1977) (hereafter referred to as the *Federal Prison Report*).

The Law Reform Commission of Canada, in its policy overview paper, *Our Criminal Law* (Ottawa, 1977), outlined the principles which should govern sentencing on pp. 24-25:

Remove all regulatory offences from the criminal regime, divert less serious real crimes outside the traditional system and there still remains a hard core of real crimes needing traditional trials and serious punishments. Here too we need restraint. For one thing, the cost of criminal law to the offender, the taxpayer and all of us must always be kept as low as possible. For another, the danger with all punishments is simply that familiarity breeds contempt. The harsher the punishment, the slower we should be to use it. This applies especially to punishments of last resort.

The major punishment of last resort is prison. This is today the ultimate weapon of the criminal law. As such it must be used sparingly. We would restrict it to three kinds of cases: (1) for offenders too dangerous to leave at large; (2) for offenders for which, as things are now, no other adequate denunciation presently exists; and (3) for offenders wilfully refusing to submit to other punishments. For these three cases prison is the penalty of last resort.

Restricting our use of imprisonment will allow more scope for other types of penalties. One penalty our system should use more extensively is the restitution order. To compel offenders to make restitution to their victims is one of the most fruitful types of punishment. It brings home to the offender the wrong he has done his victim, it meets the real needs of the victim himself, and it satisfies society's sense of justice and the desire to see that the offender is not profiting at the expense of his victim's suffering. Restitution has a vital place in any decent criminal justice system.

Equally vital is a second kind of reparation. Although one victim of a crime is the individual who is wronged, another victim is society whose values have been threatened and infringed. Society too has a claim to reparation — a claim not satisfied by "payment in the hard coinage of imprisonment." The claim is better met by more creative penalties like community service orders compelling the offender to do something positive to make up for the wrong he has done society.

Positive penalties like restitution and community service orders should be increasingly substituted for the negative and uncreative warehousing of prison.

Inside the Prison: Violence

The *Federal Prison Report, supra,* was undertaken as a result of the ongoing violence in the prison system. There were other reports which seemed to have the same thrust. But apparently they had little national effect. See, *Alberta Inquiry into the Alleged Excessive Use of Force at the Calgary Correctional Institute, Report of A. M. Harradence, Q.C.,* Aug. 23, 1973, Section 1-2:

> Confinement of human beings against their will in close proximity to each other creates an abnormal and explosive situation. Trivial incidents take on a monumental significance. Frustration and violence are the norm, and perversion is accepted. . . .
> The Commission concludes that in a Custodial Institution, the provision of meaningful work is essential to reduce and bring within control the level of tension and frustration which incarceration inevitably produces. The attainment of this objective is not to be taken as a substitute for rehabilitation. If the provision of such work demands greater expenditure on custodial capacity to control inmates while such work is carried out outside the secure portions of the Institution, such expenditures must be made. . . .
> The objectives of the concept of rehabilitation cannot be met within the custodial environment. All that can be hoped for in the custodial environment is that the inmate can be taught to live in that environment. It is rehabilitation which teaches him to live in society.

See also, *Report of the Commission of Inquiry into Certain Disturbances at Kingston Penitentiary during April, 1971,* J. W. Swackhomer, Q.C., Chairman, (Information Canada, 1973). This report discussed the relationship of the prisoner to the prison guard at pp. 39-42:

> The more ritualistic and confining are the duties of staff, the more pronounced the tendency of some to be authoritarian and punitive; moreover this phenomenon leads some correctional staff to rationalize their attitudes and behaviour on the basis of the very responses they elicit. . . .
> Correctional officers at Kingston frequently complained that they were provided with no substantial opportunity to participate in the direction and management of the institution and that major decisions directly affecting them were taken by others without any meaningful consultation, and without adequate explanation. . . .
> The classification officer is the only person to whom the inmate can turn for a broad variety of reasons relating to all aspects of his life in the institution.
> It is the intent of these recommendations to place prisoners in direct contact with staff who perform a variety of staff functions, and to whom custody and security are not matters of exclusive concern. . . .
> In order to assure that training is effective, and that the program of the penitentiary is being purposefully carried forward by all, staff meetings must

be held on a regular basis at which full and frank discussion of the penitentiary program is conducted and encouraged. . . .

Inmates in maximum security penitentiaries like Kingston are forced to live, perhaps for many years, in circumstances which are shockingly unnatural in terms of normal working, intellectual, social or sexual life. . . .

Inmate Committees of one kind or another have been in existence for almost as long as prisons themselves. Indeed, the principle that inmates may serve legitimate participatory roles in the management of certain facets of prison life is well established.

See also, Schroeder, Andreas, *Shaking It Rough; A Prison Memoir* (Toronto: Doubleday Canada, 1976). At pp. 34-35 Schroeder, who spent eight months in the British Columbia Correctional System in 1973-74 for possession of four pounds of cannabis with intent to traffick, wrote:

They call it the Prison Waltz or the Slammer Shuffle. It's that particular prison walk which is unique to inmates who have done medium or maximum security time and is like no other walk I have ever seen. It's different primarily because its purpose differs from that of a walk along an open street; the shuffle isn't intended to get anyone anywhere; it's the walk of a man going noplace. At the same time it's designed to cover a large distance, tirelessly, like the pacing of a caged animal — because that's essentially what it is.

Since pacing implies a troubled state of mind, the shuffle has other characteristics built into it as well. It's not a good thing to be visibly troubled in prison; immediate assumptions are made about one's stability, about the chances that one might be planning an escape, about one's not adapting well into the "program" etc. So the shuffle tends to make a man in some way diminuitive, in some obscure fashion nonvisible, somehow almost nonexistent. Head down and weaving slightly, eyes focused inward and arms crossed behind his back, the shuffler paces from wall to wall or gate to gate like a mechanical toy, deep in thought or functionally mindless, lost in some underwater labyrinth of his own. But since a man deep in thought might be surprised in this place, which is by definition full of the unexpected, the shuffler walks instinctively on the forward part of the foot, rocking from instep to toes, thus constantly alert in body if not in mind. I've seen prisoners walk for hours and hours in this way.

Walking in prison actually covers many of the same functions as drinking does on the outside; where a man on the street might invite a friend to join him in a cup of coffee or a beer, an inmate suggests: "Wanna walk a bit?" Often two, three or four inmates get up to walk together, and the result might reasonably be compared to the performance of a well-synchronized chorus line. In a neat even row, their paces measured and matched, deep in conversation, the walkers stride along until they arrive at the opposite wall or barrier, where, still in perfect unison, without the slightest break in rhythm or conversation, they whirl neatly around, right foot swinging forward, left up and then down and they're off again, still in perfect unison and heading for the opposite wall, where they'll turn again and come back. This, too, I have seen continue for hours, and nobody missing a step.

Here is a sampling of the regulations of the Stony Mountain Institution in Manitoba. Is it a surprise that violence can develop?

RULES REGARDING CELL MAINTENANCE November 30, 1975

Effective immediately, the following new rules will apply; any violations of these rules may result in

a. Loss of privileges
b. Poor cell ratings
c. Disciplinary action

no. 1. Blankets to the height of the fourth crossbar (approximately 50 inches from the floor) may be permitted but only during the period from 18:00 hours (6:00) to 23:00 hours (11:00). Clear plastic shields to prevent drafts may be available on request.

no. 2. Inmates are not permitted to tamper in any way with the cell light fixture.

no. 3. Cell furniture may not be moved or rearranged; it must remain as per the diagram posted on the bulletin board. The clothes closet must remain at the rear of the cell, opposite the toilet; the bed must be on the opposite side of the door opening; and the bed must be within 6 inches from the front of the cell. The toilet seat must not be removed or damaged.

no. 4. Inmates must sleep with their heads towards the front of the cell.

no. 5. An inmate may not paint or repaint his own cell.

no. 6. An area of 24 inches by 36 inches will be marked above the desk location in each cell. This area may be used for displaying pictures, photographs. THERE ARE TO BE NO PICTURES, PHOTOGRAPHS, CUTOUTS, PIN-UPS OR ANY OTHER DECORATIONS HUNG, POSTED, GLUED ON ANY OTHER AREA OF THE CELLS. (OTHER THAN THE ONE BLANKET MENTIONED IN NO. 1 ABOVE.)

no. 7. Inmates are expected to keep their own cell clean and sanitary at all times.

Reform: Questionable

Elles, Desmond, *Violence in Prisons*, (Toronto: Lexington Books, 1969); Greenway, W. K. and Brickey, S. L., eds., *Law and Social Control in Canada*, (Toronto: Prentice-Hall Canada, 1978); Helwig, David and Miller, Billie, *Story About Billie*, (Ottawa: Oberon Press, 1973); Hogarth, John, *Sentencing as a Human Process*, (Toronto: University of Toronto Press, 1971); Honderich, T., *Punishment, The Supposed Justifications*, (Don Mills: Longmans Canada, 1972), James, Lois, *Prisoners' Perceptions of Parole*, (Toronto: University of Toronto Press, 1972); Kirkpatrick, A. M. and McGrath, W. T., *Crime and You*, (Toronto: Macmillan Company of Canada, 1976); Mayeroff, Milton, *On Caring*, (Toronto: Fitzhenry and Whiteside, 1971); Waller, Irwin, *Men Released From Prison*, (Toronto: University of Toronto Press, 1978).

OVO Photo Magazine in its Summer/Fall 1976 issue published materials relating only to Canadian prisons. On page 11 William MacAllister, president of the inmate committee at Archambault Institute in Quebec, wrote of the prison strike in 1975. He said, in part:

Most strikes are to gain greater monetary sums, better pension plans, earlier retirement, less working hours, etc.; but, ours — a prison strike — was in sharp contrast; for we struck to obtain respect in the eyes of our keepers and society,

129

in the hope that this would be the origin for genuine change in a decrepit, morally bankrupt federal penal system.

It all commenced in April 1975; and like most good Beaujolais wines it matured early in body, strength and spirit with the formation of a duly elected Inmate Committee, truly representative of all prisoners.

In October 1975, we informed the Archambault Administration of our intention to strike, after obtaining a 93 per cent support vote from a general population of three hundred and sixty. The Administration scoffed and ridiculed this majority percentage; however they agreed to renewed talks on previously rejected Inmate Committee projects and temporarily averted a strike.

The next three months proved to be an exercise in total futility, as we once again encountered the same repetitious refusals attributed to a limited bureaucratic vocabulary:

LACK OF PERSONNEL: Yet the Canadian Penitentiary Service employs 9,600 people to supervise 8,700 federal Inmates, which per capita is greater than any other democratic country in the free world, to maintain our disgraceful 85 per cent rate of recidivism, compared to Sweden's 12 per cent. WHY?

SECURITY REASONS: There hasn't been an escape from this seven-year-old institution since 1972, and since that date the most modern security devices in the world have been implemented, making it a super maximum penitentiary. It's strange, when one considers an annual security budget of four million dollars is allotted for Archambault, while half of its inmates will be released within four years in accordance with the legal expiration of their sentences.

LACK OF FUNDS: They acquired the necessary funds to hire additional personnel and implement the numerous overly exaggerated security innovations. Since 1960, the penitentiary system has expanded from eleven penitentiaries to the present forty-nine, with five more on the drafting board. Excellent progress, depending on which side of the bread your butter is on, and who is paying for it!

TRY THIS ON FOR SIZE: Warden's annual salary: $31,500; Assistant-Directors': $21,500; so-called Social Workers': $15,000 to $18,000; Correctional Officers', CX 6: approx. $16,000; CX 4: $14,000 to $14,500. Yet, an educated professor teaching in Quebec, with a masters in religious science, a masters in Slavic studies, and a Ph.D. in Philosophy, who speaks seven languages and has twenty-one years of scholarity, signed his last working contract for $13,100 annually, plus a meagre 5 per cent cost of living increase.

SUGGESTION UNDER STUDY: Only one problem: it's usually an eternal study! Then there is the "Old Standby", the Commissioner's Directives, commonly referred to as the Penal Bible. The only sense Albert Einstein would derive from it would be nonsense, at best!

A key to reform, according to the *Federal Prison Report, supra,* is nothing less than a *statement of purpose.* There simply is no cohesive policy relating to the correctional system. The report concluded on pp. 155-156:

750. This point may be illustrated by the conclusion we have reached, and which was specifically stated by more than one of the many experienced and distinguished witnesses we have heard, that nothing in the criminal justice system proceeds according to any clear or generally accepted principles defining the purposes of the penal system: who should be incarcerated, and why, or what the Penitentiary Service is supposed to accomplish. Without such principles the governing ethic of what is otherwise one of the world's most

advanced and sophisticated instruments of justice is reduced to one of primitive retribution — a generalized feeling that wrongdoers ought to be punished, not because it will do them or society any good but simply because they deserve it. We cannot dignify the consequences of this as being an acceptable expression of any moral purpose. Rather they are the terrible result of a system of criminal justice that lacks the internal means for self-examination and renewal.

751. A Canadian with inmate experience, Andreas Schroeder, has put it this way: "Prison is a huge lightless room filled with hundreds of blind, groping men, perplexed and apprehensive and certain that the world is full of nothing but their enemies, at whom they must flail and kick each time they brush against them in the dark. Prison is a bare and bewildering marketplace in which the sellers and buyers mill about in confusion, neither having the remotest idea of what to buy or what to sell. Prison is a composite of all those seats in the world which are obscured by pillars and beams, and from behind which you can see neither game nor scoreboard nor attract the attention of the ice-cream man." (*Shaking It Rough; A Prison Memoir*, Doubleday Canada, 1976).

752. This fundamental absence of purpose or direction creates a corrosive ambivalence that subverts from the outset the efforts, policies, plans and operations of the administrators of the Canadian Penitentiary Service, saps the confidence and seriously impairs the morale and sense of professional purpose of the correctional, classificational and program officers, and ensures, from the inmate's perspective, that imprisonment in Canada, where it is not simply inhumane, is the most individually destructive, psychologically crippling and socially alienating experience that could conceivably exist within the borders of the country.

753. This ambivalence is itself an intrinsic element of our existing system of criminal justice — a term in which we include all individuals, institutions, governments, courts and parliaments that have been or now are involved in state intervention in the lives of those who have committed anti-social behaviour. In particular cases, measured according to its internal rules of law, its requirements for fair procedures, the tradition of impartial judges and the like, our criminal justice system is an excellent instrument. What it lacks, however, is any clear or acceptable governing conception of what we as a society intend to accomplish under the rubric of "criminality."

In almost childlike fashion a spokesman for the federal union representing prison guards called the report "unfair." He said, "They gave a lot of blame to management, but only a little to prisoners." See, the *Globe and Mail*, June 9, 1977, p. 1. See also, Michael Jackson, "Justice Behind The Walls — A Study of The Disciplinary Process in a Canadian Penitentiary," 12 *Osgoode Hall Law Journal*, 1 (1974).

Work and Release

See, working paper, "Imprisonment and Release," Law Reform Commission of Canada (Information Canada, 1975) at pp. 11-12:

Experience and research in the social sciences now make it difficult to accept with easy assurance the usual justifications for imprisonment. Generally, it is

difficult to show that prisons rehabilitate offenders or are more effective as a general deterrent than other sanctions. At the same time it is clear that imprisonment serves to separate or isolate the offender and constitutes a denunciation of the harm done. Considering this, it appears prudent to exercise restraint in imposing this criminal sanction. Imprisonment should be an exceptional sanction and should only be used for the following reasons:
  (a) to separate from the rest of society for a period of time certain offenders who represent a serious threat to life or personal security of others;
  (b) to denounce the behaviour that is deemed highly reprehensible because of its violation of fundamental values; or
  (c) to sanction offenders who wilfully fail in carrying out obligations imposed under other types of sentences.

See also the working paper, "The Principles of Sentencing and Dispositions," Commission of Canada (Information Canada, 1975) at pp. 11-12: Sagarin, Edward and MacNamara, Donald, eds., *Corrections: Problems of Punishment and Rehabilitation* (New York: Praeger Special Studies, 1973); Orland, Leonard, *Justice, Punishment, Treatment: The Correctional Process*, (New York: The Free Press, 1973).

NOTES
Chapter Six

Breaking the Crime Cycle

The case reported is found in *Her Majesty The Queen v. W.S.N.* (Ontario Provincial Court, Criminal Division, Village of Bancroft, County of Hastings) in *Community Participation in Sentencing*, Law Reform Commission of Canada, (Ottawa, 1976) at p. 167. The aftermath of the case was discovered in confidential interviews between the author and police in 1978.

Judge Clendenning has been innovative on more than one occasion. Consider this case: a defendant was charged with shoplifting goods valued at $15.75. In *Her Majesty The Queen v. N.S.L.* (Ontario Provincial Court, Criminal Division, City of Belleville, County of Hastings), *id.* at pp. 161, 164-165 Judge Clendenning handed down the following sentence:

> Firstly, you will keep the peace and be of good behaviour.
>
> Secondly, you will report monthly or as may be required by a Probation Officer.
>
> Thirdly, you will remain within the jurisdiction of the Court, and notify the Court or your Probation Officer of any change in your employment, address, or occupation.
>
> Fourthly, you will not enter nor be found in the business premises commonly referred to as M.F.M. I might add, to explain this term so that you understand it, Mr. L., a term which previously this Court has been including in Probation Orders for offences of this nature in any event, in the meeting conducted the staff of the store indicated their agreement and approval of this procedure. I also understand consideration was given to the possibility of proceedings under the Petty Trespass Act in situations where it was not a term of the Probation Order.
>
> The foregoing terms, in my view, plus the subjection to the Court process, is sufficient to satisfy the principles of reformation, rehabilitation, and deterrence as it relates to you as an individual. To some extent they are also an attempt to tailor the sentence to the individual accused before the Court, notwithstanding in many instances the lack of a pre-sentence report for the reasons previously enunciated as is the case in relation to you.
>
> I am sure if for some reason some particular problem exists, of which the Court at this point is not apprised, it will manifest itself to your Probation Officer during the reporting requirement and could be the basis for an application to vary the Order to meet the individual circumstances.
>
> In addition, the terms of the Order will act as an individual deterrent inasmuch as further participation in offences of this nature could constitute a

breach of the Order, bringing into operation Sections 664 and 666 of the Criminal Code, to which I shall later refer.

If I am correct, most of the principles of sentencing have, with these terms, been satisfied, with one exception, namely general deterrence to others who might engage in offences of this nature.

As indicated earlier, in my view, fines and/or incarceration are not the answer; however, to have no general deterrence incorporated in the sentence, given the increasing incidence of this type of offence, renders the complete sentence meaningless to the public, and to some extent places the credibility of the whole legal system in issue. It is primarily to this factor this Court has directed its introspection to attempt to incorporate terms both meaningful and relative to the nature of the offence before the Court.

Recognizing the losses and concomitant costs to society, and the reflection of those costs in the form of higher prices; recognizing also the factors enunciated earlier that only one in ten offenders are apprehended; recognizing also the availability of not only our Probation Services but the volunteer program associated therewith, this Court has decided to include one additional term.

The value of the goods, Mr. L., as indicated by the Crown Attorney, is $15.75. Reduced to simplistic factors, I take the factor of four which to some extent is a recognition that the apprehension rate may be something less than one in ten; and taking into consideration the minimum wage established in Ontario as $2.25 per hour, the Court arrives at the following.

You will perform such services, in the amount of twenty-eight hours, with such volunteer services in the Belleville area as may be designated by your Probation Officer, such services to be performed within eleven months of this date.

NOTES
Chapter Seven

Delinquency, Not Crime

The story of Rocco and Laura were taken from Calvin Becker, "Statistical Follow-up of Criminal Occurrences in Toronto Patrol Area 5411: An Examination of the Relationship between Victims and Offenders," in *Studies on Diversion*, Law Reform Commission of Canada (Ottawa: Information Canada, 1975), at pp. 192-206.

See also, Krotz, Larry (ed.), *Waiting for the Ice-Cream Man: A Prison Journal — Manitoba 1978* (Winnipeg: Converse Press, 1978). At page 39 Bob Busch, an inmate of the Brandon Correctional Institution wrote the following:

> To me the system is okay for hardened criminals like your murderers, kidnappers, rapists and violent people; but to the guy who has an alcohol problem or to a drug addict or a person who has every day life problems he shouldn't be thrown in the slammer because being inside a jail isn't going to change his problems. He's going to be the same when he gets out because he never solved his problem in jail. As far as I'm concerned there's no rehabilitation in jail because being inside is a big enough problem to live with and you can't just go to other inmates and talk your problem over with them. Sure there's your classification officer and some other people who can help, but there's too many inmates to handle. I really think the problem starts when the person is a child; he's had a bad start in life because of family problems and then welfare steps in and takes kids away. When that happens the child doesn't know what way to turn so he rebels against everything because he wants to be with his parents and that's where the biggest problem is, as far as I am concerned, because it happened to me.
>
> So then the kid ends up in foster homes and Homes for Boys so by the time he's eighteen all he knows is he's got no place to go or turn to. He starts heading for provincial jails and then finally to the pens. I think if they want to help people they should start helping them when they're young because when a person like myself goes to these kinds of places he loses trust in everyone; he gets paranoid after doing so much time, he gets institutionalized and so he keeps returning to jails because there is no one to help him solve his problems.
>
> It's easy to say but it's hard to do because when you're a kid you're just like a tape recorder; everything you learned when you were a kid stays with you till someone helps you solve the problems. But as far as I'm concerned if they don't start helping people like us there's always going to be jails and we're always

going to come back because no one cares on the outside. If there's going to be jails, they should separate the hard criminals from the person who has a family problem or booze or dope problems because they don't need jail; they need people who will care for them instead of locking them up.

Other references include: *Young People and the Juvenile Justice System: A Background Paper and Policy Statement*, Canada Council on Social Development (Ottawa, 1977); Faust, Frederick and Brantingham, Paul, *Juvenile Justice Philosophy*, (St. Paul, Minnesota: West Publishing Company, 1974); Jain, Nilima, *Aspects of Juvenile Justice in Toronto*, (Downsview: Osgoode Hall Law School, York University, 1974).

"Homes" for the Young

The 1975 confidential report referred to in this section was published in limited quantities, at high prices and in a jumbled fashion. It was published with the announced aim of generating public discussion. More likely, however, the government wanted the paper justification for a decision already made: as a matter of cost savings larger institutions would be closed, and the smaller, so-called group homes, which cost less, would be developed. See, *Report of the Ontario Interministerial Committee on Residential Services to the Cabinet Committee on Social Development* (Toronto: Queen's Printer, 1975).

Under the heading of major issues and problems this is what the report stated concerning group homes on p. 139:

1. At present correctional services group homes admit only Training School wards which tends to stigmatize them as homes for juvenile delinquents and to some extent undermines the "normalization" process.
2. Although zoning restrictions and objections by neighbours are still a problem, some improvement has been noted, partly as a result of more careful choice of location. Good relationships have been developed with schools and communities have shown an increasingly responsible attitude. There is, however, a continuing job of interpretation to be done.
3. Group homes are being tested by the Ministry as a major alternative to Training School but it will be some time yet before there is sufficient experience to determine the optimum balance of resources.
4. It is suggested that more effective service may be achieved in the larger group home by a reduction in the number of resident beds.

The reality of the government's policy was made clear several months after the confidential report was prepared. Ontario announced the closing of five relatively large juvenile institutions on April 14, 1976. Corrections Minister John Smith stated that the young would be moved to group homes. The savings to government in dollars was substantial. In the first year of closing the government would save about $1 million and in the second year, $1.5 million. See, the *Globe and Mail*, April 14, 1976, p. 5.

In the absence of controls, cohesive policies and adequately trained personnel, many of the group homes proved inadequate. Once "at home," some children found themselves evicted. On October 5, 1978, six youths removed from their group home for emotionally disturbed children by the Children's Aid Society returned and vowed to fight anyone who touched them. See, the *Globe and Mail*, October 6, 1978, at p. 1.

It is a harsh statement, but it is nevertheless true: money rather than child welfare has played a major role in shaping residential policy for the young. Conflict, when it develops, often seems to be between different levels of government as to who will pay how much of the residential bill. See, M. F. McLellan, "The Viking Homes Saga: Group Home Placements for Juveniles," 1 *Canadian Journal of Family Law* at p. 126 (January, 1978).

Shunting the young from one place to another, all in the name of protecting them, becomes a very cruel joke. In December, 1976, a Family Court judge sent a fourteen-year-old boy to a Toronto psychiatric hospital for assessment. The boy spent more than a month in the adult ward. Why? Because the doctor he was supposed to see did not know that he was there. See, the *Globe and Mail*, May 12, 1976, p. 1.

The proposed bill of rights for institutionalized children is set out in the *Globe and Mail*, September 8, 1978, at p. 4. The proposed rights are the subject of two papers sponsored by the Ontario Ministry of Community and Social Services: *Consultation Paper on Standards and Guidelines for Children's Services*, and *Children's Residential Care Facilities* (Toronto, 1978).

It is indeed difficult to see the proposed standards as a marked advance over what the law should be. Still, the proposals do improve upon a bad situation. Current practice, for example, allows home administrators to open, censor, and withhold children's mail. The proposed rules would continue to give administrators the right to open mail, but they would be denied the right to censor or withhold letters.

Not only are the proposed rules an advance for Ontario, they mark the first time that any government in North America has written comprehensive guidelines relating to the rights of children in residential facilities.

No Homes for Some

Much of the material for this section is derived from the excellent article written by Michael Valpy, "Youth at the Crossroads: Scurrilous Reports and Little Else," the *Globe and Mail*, March 5, 1973, at p. 7. The absence of facilities for the treatment of youthful offenders, however, is even more apparent in the North. There the rate of commitment to training schools runs at about ten times that of the more populous urban centres. See the *Globe and Mail*, July 20, 1978, at p. 13.

Family Court Judge William T. Little of Ontario discusses the role of duty counsel in "The Need for Reform in the Juvenile Courts," 10 *Osgoode Hall Law Journal* (August, 1972) at p. 225. See also, Paul Nejelski, "Monitoring the Juvenile Justice System: How Can You Tell Where You're Going If You Don't Know Where You Are?" 12 *The American Criminal Law Review* (Summer, 1974) at p. 9.

There is another aspect to the problem of "no homes." The adjudged juvenile delinquent is a person who is brought into contact with the province. There are substantial numbers of young people who need help and are denied

The Front Line: The Police

See Anne Scace, "Criminal Justice and Social Justice — Management of Conflict and Social Disorder by the Metropolitan Toronto Police Department," in *Studies on Diversion*, Law Reform Commission of Canada, (Information Canada, 1975) at p. 95. Of the role of the police Ms. Scace wrote at pp. 121-123:

> To propose changes in the law without due consideration of the social problem as seen by police, nor an understanding of how they exercise their discretion in applying existing law, but simply to concentrate on due process values or civil liberties can have chaotic results which may negate the theoretical basis of the desired legislation. For example, when the vagrancy statutes were removed from the Code was there any consideration of police use of those statutes? In the preparation of the recent Law Reform Commission paper on Statements and Admissibility, was any police evidence drawn on for the basis of the paper? While we lament the imprisonment of alcoholics what emphasis has the community given to providing the police with an alternative to prosecution in these cases? . . .
>
> At another level, the police sometimes feel that in attempts to reform the criminal law it is largely the loud-talking minority, radicals, or elitist lawyers that get heard. The general public is not heard. Police feel that they, more so than most groups, have a pretty good feel for what the public expects of the criminal law, yet, too often, they see the police either brushed aside or cut off from policy information and law reform. As already indicated, this feeds police alienation and, in so far as the law may not correspond with police needs and expectations, encourages police to find ways of getting around the letter of the law.
>
> Perhaps this report on some aspects of police authority and discretion will help people concerned with reform of the criminal law. Unless there is an understanding of how police decision-making operates at the meeting of law and people in trouble, criminal justice, and particularly reform of the criminal justice system, will fail to meet the needs of ordinary citizens.

See also, Michael Valpy, "Youth at the Crossroads: Call a Spade a Spade and a Child Understands," the *Globe and Mail*, April 1973, at p. 9.

Community Judges

The experience related in this section comes from a report in the January 31, 1975 issue of the *Globe and Mail*. However, it must be stressed that there is nothing particularly inventive about what was done. Native people have long had a tradition of community involvement. Among Indian nations, working with the offender, bringing that person into the community, has been described by Professors Hoebel and Llewellyn. See, Hoebel, E. Adamson, *The Law of Primitive Man: A Study in Comparative Legal Dynamics*, (Cambridge, Mass.: Harvard University Press, 1954), pp. 127-156; Karl Llewellyn, "The Anthropology of Criminal Guilt," 2 *Social Meaning of Legal Concepts* (1952), p. 100.

On pp. 109-110 Professor Llewellyn wrote of the New Mexican Pueblos:

But when one begins to observe the highly geared drive for rehabilitation of the offender which pervades Cheyenne criminal law, one begins to prick up his ears. When one turns to the New Mexican Pueblos, and finds an established system to deal with both petty and grave offences on that same basis, with punishment, as a matter of conscious philosophy, relegated to the role of an educational tool, then one does more than prick up his ears. One settles down to learn.

Here is a completely different approach to problems of criminal law. Offences are foreknown as such, so far as experience is at hand, but hitherto unprecedented offenses can be fore*felt* as such when they run clearly counter to the tone and purpose of going institutions. A trial lies half in an inquiry by officials, an inquiry reaching "real evidence" (tracks, etc.), and all available testimony, including that of the suspect or accused; what he has to say in argument or extenuation is part of this phase. The officials will go drum up evidence for him on their own or at his instance. *They want to find him innocent*: he is part of their team. What is known as the "trial," the second half of the procedure, is formal on the point of fact, except in an exceptional case. Its purpose is to bring the erring brother, now known to be such, to repentance, to open confession, and to reintegration with the community of which he *was and still is a part*. As contrasted with arm's-length attitudes, the law, the procedure, the treatment, the attitudes, the emotions are *parental*. There is infinite patience in the tribunal, infinite long-suffering. Typically, also, there is infinite ultimate inflexibility: it is the offender who will have to do all the ultimate yielding. The results, 95% of the time, make our results look weak, uncertain, costly. But when the parental system once goes wrong, the results raise the hair. Let officials turn the machinery to work out a personal grudge; or to enrich themselves corruptly; or to put down political dissent — and one begins to understand why our forefathers, through the centuries, found it worth blood to win through to measures which could partly control officials.

the attention of the province — until they offend against the law. In 1975 it was estimated that there were about 71,000 moderately to severely disturbed children in Ontario. Douglas Finlay, then acting director of children's mental health services for the Ministry of Health, estimated that only half of this number is reached. See, Kathleen Rex, "Troubled Teen-Agers with Nowhere to Go," the *Globe and Mail*, March 26, 1975, p. W1.

NOTES
Chapter Eight

Law without Policy: A Story

The story in this section was developed by Michael O'Brien of Osgoode Hall Law School. It brings together and allows us to sharpen our questions concerning the criminal law. It compels us to ask what the criminal law should be directed toward achieving.

The issue of "brain death" was dramatized in the United States by the story of Karen Ann Quinlan who was in a coma for more than three years. Her parents were successful in having her removed from life-support machinery. The question the court had to decide was one raised under the criminal law: To what extent was there criminal liability for such action? Two years after the court permitted the machinery to be removed Ms. Quinlan, then twenty-four years old, remained alive, though she was "brain dead." See the *New York Times*, April 10, 1978, at p. B3.

The Canadian position is somewhat more narrow than that of the United States. See, the *Canadian Medical Association Statement on Death* (Dec. 28, 1968), 99 *Canadian Medical Association Journal* 1266, at 1266-67:

1. Unreceptivity and unresponsiveness.
   Unresponsiveness is the basis of our presumption of unreceptivity.
2. No movement and no breathing.
   If the patient is on the ventilator, he must be given a trial of spontaneous respiration. When this is done, the blood gases should be normal and the patient should have been receiving less than 40% oxygen through the respirator. Mechanical ventilation is withheld for about four minutes, unless cyanosis becomes obvious.
3. No reflexes.
   Reflexes can be divided into two categories: (a) Brain stem and (b) spinal. The brain stem reflexes (pupillary, oculovestibular, corneal, pharyngeal and swallowing) must be lost. The spinal reflexes (myotatic jerks and plantar responses) are mediated through the spinal cord only. These may persist in the absence of cerebral control as seen in the paraplegic and it is not necessary to wait for their abolition to diagnose brain death.
4. Electrocerebral silence.
   Both the Canadian and American groups emphasize that the flag EEG provides only confirmatory evidence that the brain is dead.
5. A core body temperature above 90F or 32.2C and the absence of central nervous system depressants, particularly barbiturates. Warming the

patient or eliminating barbiturates may well revive the patient and even a flag EEG may spring into action.
6. If no cause for the coma is known, it is recommended that all tests be repeated in 24 hours.

See also, "Manitoba Law Commission Proposes to Define Death Under Any Circumstances" (Feb. 3, 1973), 108 *Canadian Medical Association Journal* 381. See also, L. Kushnir, "Bridging the Gap: The Discrepancy Between the Medical and Legal Definitions of Death," 34 *University of Toronto Faculty of Law Review* 199 (1976) at pp. 215-216:

The legal status of the brain death concept in Canada is less clear than in the United States. Although Canadian medical advancements parallel those in America, and criteria resembling the Harvard definition have been adopted by the Canadian Medical Association, comment on the resulting legal implications has been sparse. Furthermore, aside from the 1973 proposal of the Manitoba Law Reform Commission which proposed the following definition of death:

[t]he death of a person takes place at the time at which irreversible cessation of all that person's brain function occurs, and when it appears that withdrawal, if already instituted, of any artificial support of that person's vital functions causes or will cause the immediate onset of tissue disintegration throughout that person's body

there have been no legal attempts to remedy the situation. This may be partially due to the medical profession's bias against legislative intervention in an area considered its exclusive concern. Yet it is doubtful that the common law courts will tackle the definitional problem. Review of Canadian cases fails to disclose what may be termed the "traditional legal definition of death" or anything comparable to the Black's Law Dictionary definition. The issue simply appears not to have arisen in Canadian case law; nor is it likely to. The absence of contingency fees in the province of Ontario and the loser's liability for both parties' legal fees are likely to discourage potential litigants from embarking on such an uncertain course. Similarly, the Crown is unlikely to bring any criminal prosecutions where the odds favouring success cannot be previously determined. Thus, while reliance on the outdated concept of death generates the same uncertainties in Canada as in the American jurisdictions, the ameliorating influence of an active judiciary grappling with the problem is sorely lacking here. One can therefore conclude that the need for legislative action in resolving the discrepancy between the medical and legal definitions of death is even more acute in Canada.

This article has attempted to disclose how inadequate the traditional legal definition of death is to deal with the problems posed by modern medical technology and knowledge. To the extent that consensus exists on the basic factors which constitute brain death, there appears little justification for stalling legal sanction of medical realities. Although both the common law courts and the legislature are equipped to effect this legal alteration, it is the contention of this writer that the task can be most effectively accomplished via legislation following the example of the Kansas and California statutes which establish the brain death standard for determining the time of death as a matter of law. The gap between the medical and legal definitions of death is thereby bridged.

In the United States so-called "living wills" are being developed as a constructive alternative to the criminal law. That is, individuals in some states are allowed to instruct their doctors, subject to certain safeguards, to permit removal of life-support machinery on the occurrence of "brain death." See, "The Living Will — Already a Practical Alternative," 77 *Texas Law Review* at 665 (1977); "The Living Will — The Right to Die with Dignity," 76 *Case Western Reserve Law Review* at 485 (1976).

Public Policy: Defining the Criminal Law

Dr. Morgentaler put himself against the system. His story is told with considerable sympathy by Pelrine, Eleanor Wright, in *Morgentaler: The Doctor Who Couldn't Turn Away*, (Toronto: Gage Publishing, 1975). It is useful to speak of Doctor Morgentaler's personal feeling in his actual contact with the highest court of the land. See pages 145-146:

> Said Morgentaler of the moment when he walked into the Supreme Court:
> "I had a mixture of feelings. The feeling that finally, for the first time, the law was going to be questioned and challenged, and that finally, in this way, a cruel, unjust, and barbarous law that exposes women to danger, would be somehow amended or changed by judicial process. Also, of course, I hoped that the jury acquittal, since the jury system is one of the bulwarks of the British-based system of justice, would be upheld.
> "More than a sense of exhilaration, I thought, hopefully, the Supreme Court will recognize that the law itself is unjust, that it is a violation of the Canadian Bill of Rights. And hopefully, the highest court in the land will decide as I have always claimed that it is the duty of a doctor to help a person in need or distress."
> Morgentaler's hopes soon began to fade. "The contrast between my expectations and the reality of the Supreme Court — with all the old judges, some who barely listened, and the others who peppered the lawyers with impolite and downright hostile questions — was depressing. After the second day, if I had not been trying to avoid being found in contempt of court, I would have told the journalists who questioned me that, after two days of hearings, I was downright pessimistic. I felt that the judges had little concept of reality, that they were conservative, some hostile or biased, and I found it difficult to believe that I would get justice from them. Yet I still expected some remnant of justice, since I hoped that they would uphold the sanctity of trial by jury, and order a new trial. I no longer expected acquittal, but I never expected that they would uphold the reversal of the jury verdict."

Making Moral Decisions

The words of Edmond Cahn offer a democratic resolution. They point to the need for community involvement. That is the essence of this book. See, Cahn's preface to Arthur Koestler, *Reflections on Hanging* (New York: Macmillan Company, 1957). See also, Cahn, *The Sense of Injustice: An Anthropocentric View of Law*, (New York: New York University Press, 1949) at pp. 20, 27:

What powers men delegate to their governments depend upon what they think of themselves and of their needs. . . . If the citizenry thinks well of its own intelligence and wisdom, it will bridle at censorship; it will struggle for access to facts and ideas. Men who do not respect human capacity will raise no such objections. They will feel no loss in being closed out from what they cannot use. . . .

The sense of injustice is right in so far as its claims are recognized in action. Its logical justification must be found in its efficacy, for it succeeds in fact precisely to the extent that relevant circumstances have been understood, felt, and appreciated. Like other biological equipment it endures because it serves, and serves better through progressive adaptation. So despite all blunders and insensibilities, the sense of injustice is on the right side, the side of fallible men. Offering a common language for communication and mutual defense, it reduces the perils of isolation. It affords some warrant of a progressively better legal order, and thus makes law a vehicle of persuasion. Plato has said that the creation of the world is the victory of persuasion over force; the instrument of that victory is justice.

INDEX

A

Abortion
Morgentaler case 95-96

Allmand, Warren (former
Solicitor General— 68

B

Bennett, Chief Justice 40

C

Canada
Law Reform Commission of
Canada, 1976 Report 2, 5, 8,
10-11, 14-15, 31, 48, 54, 72-78
Parliamentary Sub-Committee
on the Penitentiary System
in Canada, Report to
Parliament, 1977 3-4, 58-62
Supreme Court of 96

Capital punishment
Police views of 54-56
Community view vs. decision of
legislature 95

Clendenning, Judge J. L. 72-78

Community Correctional Centres
68-69

Community involvement
"Good Samaritan" legislation
— Ontario 1
British Columbia heroin
programme 14
Police cooperation with
community 48-52, 88
Unusual sentence in Bancroft,
Ontario 72-78
Christian Island — Participation
of tribal council 89
Necessary for justice 96-98

Criminal Code 18, 32, 95

Criminal injuries compensation
boards 36-41
In rape cases 40-41

Criminal justice system
Goals of 3
Failure of 4
Lack of public understanding
of 8-10, 16-17
Overloading of 10-11, 18-20
Moral role of 14-15, 96
Profit or loss to state? 26-28
Fails to help victim of crime
22-27, 34-36
Innovative experiment in 72-78
Principles require ongoing
political examination 94
Narrow role of courts in
preventing injustice 96-98

Criminal trial
At its best 10
Average length of 10, 20

D

Drugs, including alcohol
Related offences 12-13
Heroin programme in British
Columbia 13-14

F

Fines
Imprisonment for failure to pay
11, 26-28, 58
Alternative to fine 12
Crime profitable in spite of
fines 23
Benefit to state 26
Annual amount collected in
Ontario 28

H

Haines, Mr. Justice Edson 24

I

Indians, native Canadian 2, 27, 89

J

Jaques, Emanuel 5-10

Juveniles
Juvenile Delinquents Act 80, 83
Juvenile courts 80-82, 85-87
Group homes for 81-84
Proposed bill of rights for 84
Probation for 87
Police relations with 87-88
Toronto police Youth Bureau
87-88
Required to work in
community 89

L

Law Reform Commission
(see Canada)

Legislature, role of 93-95

Linden, Mr. Justice A. M. 26, 33

M

McRuer, Mr. Justice 36-37

Metropolitan Toronto
Yonge Street Strip — Emanuel
Jaques murder case 5-7

Metropolitan Toronto police 49
Citizen complaint Bureau 49-50
Number of individual police
    contacts 49
Rape Crisis Centre 44
Police Community Service
    Officers 52-53
Youth Bureau 88

O

Ontario
    Criminal Injuries Compensation
        Board 37-41
    Royal Commission on Civil
        Rights 36-37
    Board of Parole 67
    Report on group homes for
        children 82

P

Parole 66-69, 81

Plea bargaining 11, 21-22, 31, 43,
    57-58

Police
    Number and cost of 3, 54
    Frustration felt by 42-43
    Exercise of discretion by
        45-49, 87-88
    Role in rape cases 45
    As social service agency 46-47
    Job definition of 46
    Cooperation with community
        49-51
    Public opinion of 53

Prisoners
    Number of 3, 12, 57
    Crimes for which sentenced to
        prison 58-59

Poverty of 27, 58
Wages of 36, 65
Despair of 63
Women 63-64
Institutionalization of 72-73

Prison guards
    Ratio to prisoners 3, 63
    Pressures on 60-62
    Demoralization of 61-63
    Harassment by 62

Prisons
    Cost of 3, 36, 65, 71
    Violence in 3, 59-62, 64
    Maximum security 59-62
    Failure to rehabilitate 64-65, 69

Probation 67, 74-77
    Restitution a condition of 32
    For juveniles 87

Property, crimes against 2-3, 12,
    20, 28, 58, 71

Provincial experience and cases
    British Columbia 2, 13-14, 17,
        30-31, 50-51
    Ontario 11-13, 28, 30, 37-41, 67,
        72-78, 82-89
    Quebec 29, 49, 96
    Saskatchewan 27

R

Rape 39-41
    Treatment in Britain 39-40
    Complaints of rape victims
        against courts 44

R.C.M.P. 50-51, 53

Recidivism 3, 71-77

Restitution
  Rare cases of 32-34, 75-76, 81
  Use by defence 34
  Criminal injuries compensation boards 36-41
  Proposal to integrate into criminal justice system 34-36, 41
  Required by police for juveniles 88

S

Schroeder, Andreas 63, 69

T

Temporary absences programme 66

Traffic offences 11-12, 20

U

United States National Commission on the Prevention of Violence 21

V

Victim of crime
  Lack of compensation for 22-27, 30-31
  Restitution ordered for 32-34, 75-76, 81
  Criminal injuries compensation boards 36-41
  Rape victims 39-41, 44-45

Violence
  Crimes of 17-18, 29, 51-52
  By police 29
  In prisons 3-4, 59-62, 64